When Things Go Boom!
By Brian Howard

A Highly Practical (NO FLUFF!) Guide
To What You Can Do <u>NOW</u>
To Prepare For The Coming Chaos

Techniques, Tips and Supply Checklists

www.WhenThingsGoBoom.com

Dedicated to Heather, Austin and Braden
The only reasons that I want to survive

Table of Contents

Introduction

Disaster preparedness or 'Prepping' is a term which can strike unnecessary fear and trepidation in the minds of many who wake up one morning to the realization that if something catastrophic happened around them, they would find themselves quickly on the wrong side of a bad situation. The simple fact that you have chosen to read this guide is a positive reflection on the fact that you have at least acknowledged that you need to be prepared before an emergency or disaster occurs, rather than be one of the screaming and panicking throngs of people who never stopped long enough in their busy lives to see what was falling around them. We have forever heard that the best time to prepare is before an event occurs; however, you would be surprised by the numbers of people who never put actions to that wisdom, never think of their family's safety, and never think 'What if' at all. It was a sad day when I finally had to accept in my mind that some people would never heed the warning until it was too late. It makes me wonder about those citizens of Pompeii. Did they even consider the idea that living at the base of Mount Vesuvius might not be the best idea for their health? Or did the people of Indonesia consider, after the massive earthquake in 2004, that a tsunami might be a possibility and taking higher ground was prudent? And do the people of these United States even comprehend the possibility of an economic financial collapse which could lead to chaos and panic as never experienced before? People are funny creatures. Perhaps it is a blessing to be living in these United States, or perhaps in some ways it is a curse since we have the false illusion that nothing bad can happen to us here. Why should we be concerned? We live in the land of milk and honey, democracy and freedom, a never ending supply of anything and everything. War doesn't come here, poverty and famine don't dare grace our shores, natural disasters only happen in places I can't pronounce much less give a rip about. Think again.

Well before I go on much further, I think this would be a good place to tell you a little about myself, why I do what I do, and what I believe. This is my first undertaking into the world of writing, so my writing style may or may not be favored by your literary prowess; however, I substitute my style for my passion on the subject. First let me say that I am not a loon, a crackpot, a Rambo waiting to kill someone, or a member of any bizarre religious or political cult. I do not do what I do to draw attention to myself, to bring myself wealth and riches (been holding my breath on that one), or to satisfy some wild psychosis in my brain which has yet to be diagnosed. What I am is a husband to my wonderful wife (whom I don't deserve), a father to my two wonderful sons (who bring me such joy), an unapologetic Christian conservative male who loves the Lord with all my heart (which I fail continually, but He forgives), a military veteran of these United States (for a country which I have loved but fear for our future), and a concerned individual who wants sincerely to help those who want help; and I try my best to help those who don't even know they need help.

So why do I do what I do? Good question and I am glad that you asked (or didn't). I joined the U.S. military right after the first Gulf War began in 1990 out of a deep-rooted sense of patriotism, love of country, and desire to serve and do my part. While spending most of my service in the southern mountains of Germany, I began acquiring a military mindset toward survival tactics and attention to detail which I can only look back now on with a sense of appreciation and thankfulness that I did. These things would serve me greatly later and will, I am sure, in the days and months of the future to come. Then as with many of us, September 11th, 2001 occurred and sparked an ember within us that would never go out, but rather smolder and burn until it individually decided to burst into a flame of awakening. The awakening was not that the United States would rise again, or we will destroy our enemies, or God will once again bless our country; but rather, the awakening was an awakening to the fact that the United States and the world would never ever be the same again. Something had shifted in such a monumental way that we were now on a course toward an incredibly bleak future, not just the United States, but the world and humanity as a whole. We had finally poisoned ourselves with evil, greed, debt, apathy, and plain bad choices and leadership until we were at the point of no return. A tipping point had been reached, and now we were about to barrel down the tracks at breakneck speed with the only outcome to be total collapse, eventually to be born again out of the ashes. So whether you call this the secular belief of total collapse of society out of our own ignorance and self-destructive behavior, or whether you call this the Christian belief of the End Times that have to occur before Jesus returns to complete redemption (which is my personal belief); either way, it will occur. You don't need to be a rocket scientist to look at what is happening right now in the world and see that this is indeed a true statement. The situations are culminating, the tensions are rising, and the stage is set: Are you adequately prepared? Not for what you hope will happen, not for what you deny will happen, but for what will happen. This is a question you have to ask yourself.

In 2007, I awoke. And so I prepare.

For God, Politics or Grit

Now the reasons people choose to begin preparing are varied and, quite honestly, irrelevant; however, I will attempt to break them down into three main camps: God, Politics or Grit. Some people choose to begin this journey because of religious beliefs, the End Times scenario. These people hold a multitude of beliefs that span the gambit from hell and brimstone the world is ending, to outright religious doomsday cults, to more moderate believers (the majority) that believe we are indeed within the end times as mentioned in the Book or Revelation in the Bible. They understand this is a fight between the forces of good and evil, and evil is on the final push to stop its predefined outcome. Since I have already stated my personal beliefs, I will leave you to determine which bucket I fall into. For these people, they understand the end. The only question is at what point do they get pulled out of it, and how much they will have to endure until that day? These people tend to quietly prepare, and cautiously feel each other out to find other like-minded individuals to share information with. Do not underestimate the numbers of these; there are hundreds of thousands, if not millions, and growing rapidly. The motivation behind these individuals is to help themselves and others, to explain to believers and non-believers exactly what is happening during this time, and to spread the love of their higher calling. They do it for God.

Some people could care less about religion of any sort but rather are deeply invested in the world whether financially, environmentally or politically. As markets teeter on violently shifting high wire acts; as currency's entire futures are in jeopardy; as world, national and personal debt has reached unsustainable levels, these people see and come to understand what a fragile house of cards the entire world's economies are now resting upon. Unemployment, recession, foreclosure are the buzzwords of the day, and when that first domino falls, they know they better be ready. Likewise, you have those who realize that the environment is shifting into some sort of period of traumatic earth changes. Threats of drought, tsunamis, super volcanoes, massive earthquakes, solar flares and coronal mass ejections, shifting magnetic poles, near earth asteroids and more offer a host of possible cataclysmic scenarios. Scientists will readily acknowledge and agree that these types of events have occurred in the past and will, without a doubt, occur again; however no one wants to believe it is near. They are wrong. Political turmoil is also rocking the world with the feeling of impending uneasiness. As regime after regime is toppled, wide vacuums are left in fragile political structures. Countries are positioning for limited resources, while people's lives are used as pawns in an elite power struggle. Terrorism is on the rise at the same time that political in-fighting has reached a fever pitch. A polarization is occurring among these people. They know something is about to crack, they look around for those to blame, and then they prepare for possible revolutions and outcomes. Whether they are looking at financial, environmental, political situations or more, they feel that preparation is a prudent next step. They tend to be highly educated on world events, often involved with political movements and causes, and sometime prone to conspiracy theories. Some of them are probably true. They do it for the world and politics.

And finally, you have those who just have the grit of survivalists. Even if the world was humming along and everyone had a song in their heart and a whistle on their lips, they would still prepare. This group refuses to lose control of a situation and let themselves or their families be in any perceived danger. They are planners, preparers, often loners, usually ex-military. They channel the internal Rambo; but they have something that everyone needs, an unquenchable will to survive and the skills to do so. Like the other two groups, they see what is happening. They study it, they learn from it. Their motivation is simple: family and self-interests.

The reasons behind all three groups are valid; and I share them all.

The Smell of Fear

Now, there is something that can bubble up within the deepest parts of the human soul that can take even the most physically prepared individual and render them mentally impotent: fear. Fear is an interesting element in the realm of disaster preparedness and survival. Fear will either produce one of two results in a person: it will either motivate you to take some action, or it will paralyze you to take no action - one or the other every time. Fear is a response that can never be totally eliminated but must be regulated. The best way to help regulate the possibility of fear in a crisis is to begin preparing for it well ahead of when you need it. Nothing can be more fearful than being hit blindside with a traumatic scenario that you feel helpless to control. Keeping a rational head is key to coping with events that will bring the average person to a weeping, sobbing basket case. I often kid with others, "Don't make me have to throw you out of the lifeboat!" You know the type. Sometimes you may be faced with the decision to jettison the panicking ones in order to not be dragged down to your own untimely death. These are tough decisions, but ones that you must be prepared for and be willing to make. When we are talking about survival, we are talking about just that, survival. Our goal should always be to ensure our family's survival with the least amount of trauma and with the bulk of our humanity intact. But understand this, those who mean to do you harm can smell fear from a long way off, and that is a smell which they are highly attracted to. Therefore, whomever you have chosen or delegated to act as leader of your group, make sure they have a cool, calm, decisive head on their shoulders. I pray (yes people, I pray) that when the time comes, I will handle myself in that manner.

Prayer and preparation make good bedfellows.

Order out of Chaos

Now the crisis in New Orleans during Hurricane Katrina should have been a wakeup call to many. Unfortunately, the reality is that crisis brings chaos. Katrina could have played out as just a routine hurricane strike with severe flooding, but it didn't. What we should have learned from this is that when there is a loss of control, or even a perceived loss of control, large numbers of people (a better term would be, thugs) will rise to attempt to take advantage of the situation. This occurred even before there was any desperation for food or water or other vital needs. Riots broke out the second they felt they could get away with it. Vandalism, violence and criminal behavior ran rampant. Even in a single city with the full power and resources of the country behind it, order could not be kept and authority and logistical structures quickly broke down. Police and fire fighters abandoned their posts, military units had a hard time responding, and of course, politicians were just that, politicians. Now this was just a single city. Suppose the event was much bigger and over a much larger geographical region. What then? Are you just going to stand there yelling, "Help me. Help me."? Anyone who is relying on the government to help them during a wide spread catastrophe is a fool, and a fool and his life are soon parted.

At the initial phases of a severe crisis, chaos begins as a moderate whisper. At this point, people aren't dying of starvation or dehydration necessarily; they are just taking advantage as stated above. However, as time goes on, this whisper turns into agitated griping. This is when people need medical attention that they are not getting, stomachs are going without food, and threats to safety are becoming all too real. They begin to comprehend that there is no one who is coming to rescue them, and they are on their own. Then true chaos comes into play as a shout. This is the point at which armed gangs begin taking what they need, wide-scale criminality ensues, and people show the worst sides of humanity. Bad things, very bad things begin to happen. This isn't anything new folks, there are many examples throughout history and unfortunately, history repeats itself.

The true survivor needs to make order out of this chaos.

Mobility Matters

One of the first major mistakes that people often make in preparing is to assume that your home is your last stand, so to speak. They therefore begin collecting supplies and placing them all over their dwelling, a little bit here and a little bit there with very little thought to organization or planning. While this might be adequate in a few mild situations, suppose an evacuation order is given, martial law is declared, or safety and health are greatly jeopardized by staying in place. One must never make the assumption that they can stay where they are: they must always plan with mobility in mind. The rule of thumb that I adhere to is that I could be totally on the road with all necessary supplies within the span of thirty minutes of notice, with no hopes of ever returning. How I prepare, what I prepare, and how everything is organized is done with this parameter in mind. As common wisdom suggests; it is better to prepare for quick mobility and not have to use it rather than be forced to leave and not have anything but the proverbial shirts on your backs. Hope for the best, prepare for the worst.

In order to accomplish this goal of mobility, one needs to procure an enclosed trailer of adequate size and an escape vehicle that has the capability of towing it. With a few exceptions, which will be detailed later, all supply storage should revolve around this trailer so that supplies are readily available and can be quickly transported. This trailer should be secured and hidden from common view (stored in garage, shelter or other secure area), so as not to broadcast what you are doing or what valuable items lie within it. Now for those who live outside of any large metropolitan area, such as a farm or rural community, sheltering in place has a lot more potential for long-term success. However, one must still not rule out the need for mobility. Since we are talking about mobility for yourself, your family and supplies, it is vital that the vehicle which you plan to use is in excellent working order, properly maintained, and adequate for the task at hand.

Even for die hard preppers, the decision as to when to leave one's dwelling and head out to another location is a difficult one and highly debated. Given that there are numerous variables in that decision and since it really is a personal decision that must be weighed for oneself, I will leave it at that. However, prepare for it, and once you have determined that the time is necessary or right, take action.

Timing can be everything.

Practical, Practical, Practical

The purpose of this book was simple: We don't need any more books which give you a couple good tips and some information which is theory and usually not implemented; we need practical meat. So many works out there are simply fluff on the subject. They may contain one good tip on a page of otherwise useless information. Well, you have just finished reading all the fluff that is going to take place in this book, the introduction. From this point forward, all I want to give is highly practical information including techniques, tips and item checklists that can be used today, not tomorrow, so that you can be adequately and reasonably prepared for whatever chaos follows. This is not a survival techniques book; however, we do have some of that included; but this is an 'I just realized I'm not prepared, what do I need to do, and what supplies do I need to get?' kind of book. Most authors on the subject will try to give you broad ideas of what supplies you will need so that you can make your own decisions, eventually if ever. Well, what that usually means is nothing gets done. Would you rather be given broad ideas so that you are tasked with doing all the research? You could be running out of time. I am going to leave out anything that I do not feel is very practical or useful. I am not going to quote statistics or others who claim to be experts on the subject, or bog the book down in unnecessary illustrations or pictures, but give you information that I have tested and used, and products which I own and trust my life and the life of my family with. If I mention particular models or brands, then that means I am highly recommending them. If I do not mention anything specifically, then just use your judgment and get what you are comfortable with and can afford. But remember, we are talking survival gear, don't get cheap low-quality junk. You bought this book for my opinion and experience; use it. I have already put hours and hours of research into this and put this through my tests in the field. You need to understand; preparation is not only having survival items but knowing how to use them. That will take practice. We don't know exactly what is going to happen or when; but I am telling you, something big is on our doorstep. Don't be one of those preparers who always think there is tomorrow to begin or finish preparing. Preparation is continuous and ongoing, but something that must be started now and undertaken with a sense of extreme urgency. There is a name for people who have not prepared both mentally and physically. They are called 'victims' or 'casualties' and you don't want to be one of them.

Procrastination can kill. Now let's get to it!

I have broken down preparation into seven main areas that are critical to preparation and survival: personal defense/safety, water/filtration, food/nutrition, shelter/habitat, medical/first aid, communications/navigation/signaling and general.

Ch 1 - Personal Defense / Safety

While none of the other chapters are placed in any kind of particular order of importance, Personal Defense/Safety was intentionally placed first, given that without this, you may as well lay down this book now and go eat a pizza in relative bliss and ignorance. Self-preservation is a powerful force which will be used by you to protect yourself and loved ones, while at the same time possibly being used by others to commit crimes of desperation in a survival situation. Even good people can be driven to commit very bad acts when they are faced with fear, uncertainty and the need for basic life giving necessities. These people are your neighbors and others that you see every day on the street. We will not judge them since you could easily be one of them if you have not adequately prepared. The bottom line is that in desperate times, people do desperate things.

Then there are those who just are criminals at heart, who long for the day that they can take advantage of the chaos of the situation. They are opportunity hunters and will quickly form into gangs of thugs who potentially will rob, rape and even kill you simply because they can get away with it. These are the lowest form of humanity, along with terrorist elements who indiscriminately kill for political or religious reasons. To this group, it is simple: you are either victor or victim, the choice is yours. This was clearly evident in New Orleans during Hurricane Katrina.

With both of these groups the threats are real. Do not make the mistake of thinking that someone else is going to look after your personal defense. Look in the mirror; that is who is going to have to step up and protect yourself, your family and your property. The government, the police, the military may not be available to assist or perhaps even exist at all. Ok, now I have to address the pacifists out there. If you are one of those who refuse to even entertain the idea that you might have to use any kind of force to defend yourself; well, all I can say to you is that you are more than welcome to beg, plead, hug or sing to your violent perpetrators if you wish but the rest of the chapter is not for you. The only advice I can give to you is hide and hide well.

Techniques

Choosing Firearms

Choosing firearms is a highly subjective subject. Everyone has a definite opinion on what is best. So do I. And since this is my book, rather than list every single option out there which would take a book by itself, I am going to just tell you what I depend upon and what I suggest for my own family. You can take it or leave it, but these suggestions are of excellent firearms which have been proven in the field by me and others over the years. I would also advise that you have at least one firearm in each of the categories below; two of each would be even better to provide a secondary capability and also serve as a backup weapon should your primary fail or you need spare parts.

Pistol - When it comes to defense, one of the front line weapons of choice will always be the pistol. When choosing a pistol, remember that it will not only be used by you, but may need to be used by others including family members. Therefore, we want to choose something that is easy to handle, is proven, easy to maintain, and uses a caliber which is in high supply and relatively inexpensive. Given that you may or may not have your concealed handgun license, size may be an issue so that it can be concealed easily in a waistband, purse, fanny pack, etc. With regards to weapons choice, I would suggest the Beretta 92FS 9mm and the Springfield XD 9mm. For a small pocket pistol in the .22LR caliber, I would suggest the Beretta Bobcat or the Bersa Firestorm Conceal Carry Pistol.

Rifle - The category of rifle is an easy choice for several reasons. The two rifles I am going to recommend, one for primarily hunting small game and the other for combat scenarios, are the mainstays of any true preppers' arsenal. First, I would highly recommend the Ruger 10/22 (.22LR). This is an excellent choice with many options to customize for your own preferences and is probably the most used and depended upon .22LR on the market. This rifle is excellent for small game such as squirrels, birds and rabbits and the ammunition is dirt cheap. The second rifle I am going to recommend, I know better than most of my closest friends, the Bushmaster AR-15. What can I say about this weapon other than it has been used by the U.S. Military for many decades and is obviously battle proven. Obviously, since it is still the primary weapon of the military and police forces in this country today, the supply and availability is the largest out there. This is very convenient if you need to pick up a spare part or rifle from a fallen warrior in a defensive situation. The AR-15 uses the .223 caliber ammunition and can be used quite effectively for hunting as well as for personal defense. If I am going to have only one weapon by my side, this is it. Know it, love it, and learn it. A final rifle which I want to mention, is a 9mm rifle, the Hi-Point 995TS. Having a 9mm rifle is worth mentioning because it shares common ammunition with your pistol, but affords you much greater accuracy than you could achieve with a shorter barrel pistol. I have been very impressed shooting this weapon, and it would make a great secondary tactical choice. I have been able to achieve placing 20 rapid-fire rounds through a single 2-inch hole at 25 yards with no scope, just open sights with this weapon.

Shotgun - Probably one of the most frightening sounds a perpetrator can hear is the sound of a pump shotgun chambering a shell. Priceless. For blowing big holes in something at short distances, nothing compares to a 12 gauge shotgun. When it comes to this category of firearm, I am only interested in tactical uses; therefore, only five particular shotguns come into my mind: the Mossberg 930 SPX, the Mossberg 590A1, the Remington 870 Tactical, the Benelli SuperNova Tactical and the Benelli M2 Tactical. All five of these are rock solid weapon systems and pack a devastating punch.

Scopes, Lights, Night Vision and Lasers - Firearms, especially tactical, come with an endless supply of possible accessories. I am not going to go into much detail on these since they are so varied; however, I will suggest some quality companies when it comes to weapon scopes, lights, night vision and lasers. For tactical scopes, I recommend Leupold, Nikon, Trijicon or EOTech. For weapons lights, I recommend Insight, Surefire or Streamlight.

And finally, for night vision: ATN; and for lasers: Crimson Trace. These companies produce high quality products and should suffice nicely for any choice in firearms.

DON'T FORGET the AMMUNITION - Ok folks! What do you call a firearm without adequate ammunition? A club! Do not overlook the need for adequate ammunition. For the weapons that I have suggested, I have included a table below which recommends some excellent and proven ammunition for personal defense.

Ammo Recommendations		
Caliber	Manufacturer	Detail
12 gauge	Federal	#1 Buckshot
	Winchester	#1 Magnum Buckshot
	Winchester	#00 Buckshot
9mm	Federal	Hydrashok 147g JHP
	Speer	Gold Dot 147g GDHP
.22	Remington	Yellow Jacket
.223	Hornady	TAP 75g
	Federal	55g JSP

Please keep in mind; these are ammunition suggestions for your go-to-battle ammo. For practice, plinking and some bulk ammunition purposes, go with cheaper but still good quality loads. Anyone at a sporting goods or gun store can point you in the right direction. With regards to how much ammo is enough, this is a highly subjective opinion; but for 12 gauge, I would say a minimum of 500 shells; for 9mm, a minimum of 2000 rounds; for .22, a minimum of 5000 rounds; and for .223, a minimum of 2000 rounds.

Other Defense Tools

Stun Gun or Stun Baton - A stun gun or baton is excellent for disorienting and temporarily disabling a threat in close proximity to yourself. This is also able to be used against an attacking animal such as a guard dog. Also keeping in mind that you may not have an electrical power source, it would be advisable to use a battery operated model rather than a rechargeable unit. When it comes to brands, I would stick with either Stun Master or Streetwise at 400,000 volts or above.

Pepper Spray or Pepper Grenades - Pepper Sprays can be a great defense to disorient and temporarily blind a perpetrator, allowing you needed time to make an escape. When it comes to pepper spray, make sure you get at a minimum of 10% Oleoresin Capsicum (O.C.). As opposed to a stun gun, pepper spray gives you the added benefit of being able to keep a slight distance between you and the recipient. With regards to brand, Fox and Sabre are both top quality products. Fox also offers pepper grenades which are excellent for clearing an enclosed area of animals or threats.

Retractable Metal Baton - This is an excellent tool for fighting off an attacker or for breaking windows, small objects or kneecaps. These can extend up to 26 inches and will collapse down to a very small size, saving room in your bag. I would give you several brands for this, but in my mind there is only one true heavy-duty, quality brand, and that is ASP.

Baseball Bat - Never underestimate a good old-fashioned Louisville slugger to be able to inflict severe bodily harm to a perpetrator. Given the correct swing, it is amazing how damaging a piece of lumber can be. Baseball bats come in two different types: wood or aluminum. The choice between wood and aluminum is a personal one; however, keep in mind that wood will tend to crack or break first; whereas, an aluminum bat has the disadvantage of being a little heavier usually but will not break nearly as easy. Also, a wooden bat can be modified with a few, well place long nails to become a devastating club or mace. While this can be used as a defensive weapon if needed, it can also be used for hunting or fishing. Batter up.

Handcuffs - Once an individual is subdued and needs to be restrained, handcuffs are the next obvious choice. Metal handcuffs are very strong and when used properly are very difficult to remove. However, with metal handcuffs there comes a very small key which tends to get lost, and metal handcuffs are single purpose in nature. They are excellent when needing to secure an individual to an immovable object thereby limiting their mobility. The best quality brand of metal handcuffs is Smith & Wesson. Another alternative is to create your own makeshift handcuffs using zip ties. Zip ties are like duct tape in the sense that their uses are virtually limitless. Zip ties can be used in many other areas of survival; therefore, why not utilize them for restraint as well. My preferred method of securing hands is to utilize three zip ties as follows:

1. Secure a zip tie around one of the wrists and pull it very securely so that it cannot be slipped out of, but where it does not totally cut off circulation.
2. Take a second zip tie and do the same around the other wrist.
3. Now with a third zip tie, run it under each of the other ties and pull it as securely as you can, pulling the two wrists as closely as possible.
4. You can then cut off any excess tie length if needed.

Knives - Knives are an essential survival item without question. They come in all sizes and styles, and will obviously cut, kill or maim. A pocket knife should be in everyone's primary bugout bag; however, for defense purposes a tactical survival knife should have a blade of at least 6 inches. With regards to recommended brands of pocket and tactical survival knives, they would have to include Kershaw, SOG, Gerber and Ka-Bar. Knives are a highly personal choice, and as long as you stick with a dependable and quality brand, you can't go wrong. One particular knife worth mentioning for basic all-around backwoods survival is the Mora Bushcraft Survival Knife out of Sweden. This knife is highly rugged with an exceptionally sharp blade. It is great for carving and splitting wood and is relatively inexpensive.

Compound Bow or Crossbow - When you need to take care of business but you can't afford to make much noise, a compound bow or crossbow might just be what you need. They are very accurate in the right hands at short to medium distances. Many hunters are already experienced at the bow, so a simple switch of targets in not that big of a stretch. Like firearms, these are multi-purpose weapons which can be used for hunting game as well as defense. The brands that I recommend in this area are Bear and Martin for compound bows, and Barnett and Excalibur for crossbows.

Tips

Basic

- Choose ammunition calibers that are most prevalent and readily available, such as .22 LR, .223, 9mm and 12 gauge. These rounds are relatively inexpensive, in high supply, and commonly used by military and law enforcement.
- Try to limit the number of different calibers you are stocking for ammunition. It is better to have a large supply of a fewer common calibers than to have a small supply of many less known calibers.
- Don't buy a firearm unless you are willing to be trained and willing to use it if necessary.
- Always keep your knives sharp and clean, and your guns oiled.
- When purchasing firearms, take into consideration that others may be firing the weapon as well, including spouses and children if necessary.
- Make sure you have plenty of spare magazines for your firearms.
- Get a pellet gun too. While it doesn't make a good personal defense weapon, it is quiet and can take small game. It can also be used for target practice.

- In the realm of personal defense items, guns usually win.
- Dry your knife if wet before returning it to its sheath.
- Learn to use your iron sights on your firearms rather than always relying on scopes.
- Get the flat-top model of the AR-15 in order to utilize advanced optics and scopes.
- Have maintenance kits and cleaning supplies to accommodate each weapon system.

Do Now!

- If you are legally eligible to do so, consider getting your concealed carry handgun license.
- Get yourself, your spouse and your age appropriate children out to the gun range and start getting them familiar with handling and using a gun. This can be a great family activity.
- Sharpen your knives and lightly oil them.
- Find as many like-minded individuals and families that will work together, plan together, and defend together in an emergency. There is strength and protection in numbers. That is not just an old saying. It is true.
- Take a self-defense course. This is excellent for all ages, and women will find it particularly useful and comforting.

Checklist

Personal Defense / Safety Items

(In no particular order)

o Pistol(s) (Beretta, Springfield or Bersa)
o Rifle(s) (Bushmaster, Ruger or Hi-Point)
o Shotgun(s) (Mossberg, Remington or Benelli)
o Stun gun or baton (AA battery only)(Stun Master or Streetwise)
o Pepper spray (at minimum 1 small unit in each person's bugout bag)(Fox or Sabre)
o Retractable metal baton (ASP)
o Baseball bat (wood or aluminum)
o Box of 5 inch galvanized nails
o Handcuffs (Smith & Wesson)
o Zip ties (14 inch, 120 lb)(at least 100)
o Wire snips
o Knive(s) (Kershaw, SOG, Gerber, Mora or Ka-Bar)
o Knife sharpener
o Compound bow or crossbow (Bear, Martin, Excalibur or Barnett)
o Weapon scope(s) (Leupold, Nikon, Trijicon or EOTech)
o Weapon light(s) (Insight, Surefire or Streamlight)
o Night vision (ATN)
o Weapon laser(s) (Crimson Trace)
o Weapon cleaning kits
o Ammo boxes
o Desiccant
o AMMUNITION (Federal, Winchester, Speer, Remington or Hornady)

Ch 2 - Water / Filtration

In a crisis situation, clean drinkable water is one of the most important needs for human survival. People can survive for weeks or even months without food; however, survival without water is counted in days. A basic rule of thumb is that even in ideal environments, a person needs at least two quarts of clean water per day to stay in prime physical condition. This is supposing mild temperatures, little physical activity and little loss from sweating. The higher the temperature, the greater the need for higher water consumption. For people who are highly active or in excessively hot or cold temperatures, they can need more than one gallon of water a day. Water consumption is vital to the health of the circulatory and respiratory systems as well as aiding in the digestive processes. Dehydration can quickly cause the heart to be labored and lead to the loss of physical and mental abilities. When faced with a water conservation scenario, it is advisable to limit the intake of meats and salty food since they require water for digestive processing. The following chart shows a reasonable estimate of the number of days a healthy person could expect to survive, given the total amount of water to be rationed for drinking purposes.

Max. Daily Temp	Number of Days in the Shade					
	No Water	1Q / .95L	2Q / 1.9L	4Q / 3.79L	10Q / 9.46L	20Q / 18.93L
120F / 49C	2	2	2	2.5	3	4.5
110F / 43C	3	3	3.5	4	5	7
100F / 38C	5	5.5	6	7	9.5	13.5
90F / 32C	7	8	9	10.5	15	23
80F / 27C	9	10	11	13	19	29
70F / 21C	10	11	12	14	20.5	32
60F / 16C	10	11	12	14	21	32
50F / 10C	10	11	12	14.5	21	32

Q = Quarts   L = Liters

Contaminated water can contain four things that pose a substantial health risk. They include protozoan parasites, bacteria, viruses and poisonous chemicals. Protozoa include Giardia and

Cryptosporidium. These are the largest of the three pathogen categories and range in size from 1 to 16 microns. Bacteria include E. Coli and salmonella and range in size from .2 to 10 microns. Viruses, such as Hepatitis and Rotavirus are the smallest of all and range in size from .02 to .085 microns. The final category, poisonous chemicals, are not organisms but can severely damage the immune systems and other functions of the human body. Unless all four of these are protected against and removed from the water, it cannot be considered 100% safe to consume.

Water needs are divided into two categories: potable water (used for drinking, hygiene and cooking) and non-potable water (used for sanitation disposal, irrigation and other uses). Water filtration, disinfection and purification are only needed in order to render a water source potable. However, one must account for the other needs as well. A chart in the section on the storage of water will show you just how much water we are talking about and you may be shocked. It makes you appreciate when the taps are flowing and understand a little better the challenge ahead for when they are not.

Techniques

Acquiring Water

Rivers, Lakes and Streams - These are the most obvious sources of water acquisition and should be exploited whenever possible for non-potable uses as well as potable, provided that filtration/disinfection techniques are applied. We are not going to include ocean water as a source since desalinization is a complicated technique, is not practical in most emergency situations and runs a great risk if done incorrectly.

Rain Barrels - This is a good old-fashioned standby and collects rainwater naturally as it is funneled down into a single collection point. These are often placed under the downspout of the gutters along the roof of a house. This is a good method to collect water in a hunker-down-at-home situation, but since I am always focused on the portable, it also can be useful and able to transport when empty. These usually come in 55+ gallon capacity, but do not overlook the method for much smaller units of collection. Anything from buckets to pots and pans can serve in the same capacity, so the name of the game is when you are able to collect water, collect it in any way you can given what you have on hand.

Tarps, Plastic Sheeting or even Kiddie Pools - The idea is to provide the largest surface area to collect the most naturally occurring rainwater which can then be collected and used. Some examples of this include tarps and plastic sheeting which can be spread out or tied with a lower single point of exit and can then be placed above a water collection device such as a barrel or bucket. Plastic kiddie pools are also excellent since they just need a little personal air to set up and when collapsed are easy to pack quite nicely into a backpack.

Tree Sweat (Transpiration) - This process is quite simple and yet can save your life in an emergency situation. All you need for this is several clear plastic bags, a bit of cloth and a twist tie or cord. You can place several of these on a tree simultaneously to increase your yield. For this process to work, simply slip a clear plastic bag over the end of a branch of a non-poisonous tree. Where you would normally gather the bag at the open end to tie it, wrap a 1 inch, thick strip of cloth tightly around the tree limb. Clamp the bag around this cloth and use a twist tie or chord to tie it tightly together creating a tight seal. You have now basically created a greenhouse. As the sun shines through the bag, the temperature will rise causing the tree to release water vapor which will then condense at the lowest point inside the bag. After leaving it there for a day, untie the bag and gather the accumulated water. Repeat as often as needed. If I am using this method, I often use at least 1 to 2 dozen bags at a time and rotate the trees that I am using each day.

Melting Snow - This is exactly what it sounds like. If you live where there is snow on the ground, you have water. Gather up as much snow as possible (ice is even better since it is more dense) in a container and place near a heat source. Once it has melted, treat it as you would any other contaminated water source and apply the appropriate filtration/disinfection technique. Do not eat snow or ice without melting first.

Dew Collection - This can require quite a bit of effort for small results in water collection; however, in a desperate situation even a cup or two of water can mean the difference between life and death. Early in the morning, strap a highly absorbent towel such as the legendary ShamWOW to your shins and walk through a grassy field. When the towel has been saturated with dew, simply wring out into a water collection device.

Inside Structure Sources - Right inside your home or dwelling, you have a certain amount of stored water which you might not be aware of. Obviously, if the tap is still running, use it first; however, if the water supply is no longer flowing, your water heater and toilet might gain you a little bit of usable water. Most housing water heaters contain at least 75 gallons of water within their tanks. First, make sure that all power is cut off from your water heater, whether that is electricity or gas. Then turn off the flow valve, stopping all flow into the heater. Attach your garden hose to the spigot which is usually located at the base of the water heater, and place the other end of the hose into your collection device. Keep in mind you may have upwards of 75 gallons which will try to flow from the unit, so make sure you are ready to receive that amount. Finally, either open the pressure relief valve on the top of the tank, or turn on the hot water at the faucet inside the home. This will allow the water to flow once you open the spigot. So now open the spigot and collect the water, but realize this could be extremely hot water. The other in-home water source is the tank (not the bowl) of the toilets. This can contain up to seven gallons of water. As with all of these sources, assume contamination and take steps accordingly.

Swimming Pools and Spas - Outside your home, you may have two very large sources of water. Both of these should be considered non-potable use only, except in the case of a spa which had been drained and cleaned and was filled at the last minute without the addition of any chemicals. In this case, you can consider it contaminated water which can be made potable through filtration/disinfection/purification processes. In a crisis situation, swimming pool water can be used to drink if it has been boiled and treated with bleach, but only as a last resort.

Making Water Safe To Drink

Boiling - A simple boiling of suspect water for a period of one minute is more than adequate to destroy disease causing organisms and render the water drinkable. If you are at an altitude above 2000 meters/6560 feet, then expand this time to three minutes. This is the best method; however, it requires the use of a heat source, can be time consuming, and is impractical for large amounts of water. It will, however, kill all pathogens, including viruses and needs no special equipment. For best results, cloudy water should be filtered before boiling by using coffee filters, paper towels or a cheese cloth. After boiling, let water cool before drinking.

Altitude	Minutes of Boiling
Below 1000m/3280ft	1
1000m/3280ft to 2000m/6560ft	2
Above 2000m/6560ft	3

Liquid Clorox Bleach - This is a chemical disinfection process used to purify water and render it drinkable. Bleach must contain 5.25% sodium hypochlorite without soap or phosphates. Bleach should be added to contaminated water in the amounts given (generally 8 drops of bleach to each gallon of clear water or 16 drops for cloudy water). The water should be left to stand for a period of 30 minutes after the addition of the bleach. After treatment, the water should have a slight chlorine odor; if it does not, repeat the dosage and allow the water to stand an additional 15 minutes or so. If at any time the water has too strong of a chlorine taste, you can let the water stand for a longer period or aerate the water by pouring it back and forth between two containers.

Iodine - This is a chemical disinfection process used to purify water and render it drinkable; however, the bleach process is preferable over the iodine method since iodine does not break down and some people could have allergic or negative reactions to iodine solutions. As a general rule, add 5 drops per 32 oz (1 liter) of clear water, or 10 drops per 32 oz (1 liter) of cloudy water. Iodine will give the water a noticeable bitter taste. Wait at least 30 minutes before drinking water. Dropping a vitamin C tablet into the water will help remove the bitter iodine taste and also give you necessary vitamin C nutrition.

	Types of Chemical Disinfection			
Amounts	Iodine (clear water)	Iodine (cloudy water)	Bleach (clear water)	Bleach (cloudy water)
1 quart	3 d	6 d	2 d	5 d
1 gallon	19 d	38 d	1/4 t	1/2 t
5 gallons	1 1/2 t	3 t	1 t	2 t
10 gallons	1 tb	2 tb	1/2 tb	1 tb
55 gallon drum	+	+	1/4 c	1/2 c
200 gallons	+	+	1 c*	1 1/2 c*
500 gallons	+	+	2 1/4 c*	3 1/2 c*
1000 gallons	+	+	5 c*	8 c*
3800 gallons	+	+	1 g*	1 1/2 g*

d = drops t = teaspoons tb = tablespoons c = cups g = gallons

* These estimates are for initial treatments of these volumes. Regularly used water from large tanks should be treated once or twice a month at the rate of 1 oz of bleach per 200 gallons or 5 oz of bleach per 1000 gallons.

+ Not recommended for large volumes.

Solar Water Disinfection (SODIS) - This is a disinfection process, using the power of the sun along with a simple plastic bottle, to remove 99.9% of living organisms. The process is as follows:

1. Find or take a clean, clear 2-liter soda bottle and remove any labels. Make sure the bottle is free from heavy scratches and anything that would lessen its clarity for the sun to shine through.
2. Fill the bottle about 3/4 full with clear water (or pre-filtered water using coffee filter, cloth, etc).
3. Shake bottle vigorously for at least 30 seconds to highly oxygenate the water. (IMPORTANT)
4. Fill the remainder of bottle with water and securely place cap on bottle.
5. Place bottle in direct sunlight for 6 to 8 hours, and if at all possible, place bottle on some highly reflective surface such as tin foil, sheet metal or lightly colored pavement.
6. If water was cloudy when beginning or the sunlight was only partial, leave bottle in sun for a full 2 days.
7. Water should now be disinfected and drinkable with 99.9% of living organisms destroyed.

Portable Water Filtration/Purification Devices - This is by far the broadest category of ways to create safe drinking water and, arguably, the most important. Faced with a situation of being on the move and not being able to carry gallons of bleach with you, or having a readily available heat source, or having the time to use SODIS; a portable water filtration device that can be stored easily in a backpack is a mandatory and necessary item in my book. There are literally hundreds of these items out there; however, I am including only the ones that I personally trust my life with and the life of my family. I am not going to go into detail on how to use each of these items; they come with instructions for that. However, I will list the ones that I personally own and recommend and let you make your own decision on which device you choose. I do recommend looking at multiple devices rather than a single device. These are the best of the best as far as I am concerned and provide different advantages.

And yes, they are all highly portable.

	Types of Water Filtration/Purification Devices			
Device	Smallest size removed	Removes bacteria protozoa	Removes viruses	Volume capacity
Katadyn MyBottle	.3 microns	X		26 gallons
Katadyn Pocket Filter	.2 microns	X		13000 gallons
LifeSaver Bottle	.015 microns	X	X	1585 gallons
LifeSaver Jerrycan	.015 microns	X	X	5283 gallons
LifeStraw	.2 microns	X		264 gallons
SteriPEN	UV Treatment	X	X	1000 gallons
Sawyer Complete Water Purifier System (4 L)	.02 microns	X	X	1 million gallons

Katadyn, LifeSaver, LifeStraw, SteriPEN, Sawyer

Storing Water

Short-term Storage (ST) - This can be water that you plan on utilizing within the next few days or weeks.

Long-term Storage (LT) - This is for water that you plan on keeping as reserve to be used in the weeks and months to come.

The following items can be used for water storage, either on a short-term basis, long-term or both.

- Pots, Pans and Buckets (ST)
- Packaged and Sealed Bottled Water (LT)
- 2-Liter Soda Bottles (ST)(LT)
- Bathtubs and Sinks (ST)
- 5 Gallon Collapsible Water Cans (ST)
- Kiddie Pools (ST)
- Rain Barrels (ST)
- Trash Cans (ST)
- 30-55 Gallon Plastic Water Storage Barrels (LT)
- Water Storage Tanks (LT)

Remember that all water needs to be made safe to drink prior to consuming. Any amount of water from untreated sources that is going to be sealed up for a period of time should be cleaned and pre-filtered first. Long-term water supplies should be stored only in FDA approved containers. This water should also be treated with bleach (4 drops of bleach per gallon of water) prior to being stored away. All water supplies should be recycled at least every 6 months unless treated with a preserver.

When it comes to the amount of water that needs to be stored, that is a judgment call; however, you need to gain an understanding of how much water we will need to use on a day-to-day basis. You will quickly see why this can become a subject of immediate concern and importance. The following chart shows an estimate (in gallons) for a single person over various periods of time. The volumes are divided out into both potable and non-potable water.

	Water Needs Estimate (gallons)		
Number of Days for Single Person*	Potable Water	Non-potable Water	Total Volume
1 Day	2	3	5
3 Days	6	9	15
1 Week	14	21	35
2 Weeks	28	42	70
1 Month	60	90	150

This is a straight correlation; therefore simply multiply these estimates by the number of persons needed. These are very strict estimates and situations vary. However, this is assuming the potable water will be used for drinking and cooking; and the non-potable water will be used for a single toilet flush per day. A minimal shower using the excess potable water would be taken either once every three days or once a week. These estimates imply extreme water conservation.

Tips

Basic

- Given the choice between two still water ponds in the outdoors: one with algae, mosquitoes and other organisms growing in it; and the other that appears clear but has no signs of life, choose the first, since the second doesn't seem to support life and may be poisonous or chemically contaminated.
- Always assume in time of disaster that water not purchased or stored is contaminated.
- If you have no water then you should not eat at all.
- As a general rule, clear water is better than cloudy water and flowing water is better than still water.
- Even clear, cold water can be riddled with disease.

- It is always advisable to first filter cloudy water or water with particulate in it through a coffee filter, paper towel, cloth, old sock or other pre-filtering medium prior to the primary filtration/disinfection procedure.
- If using the SODIS method of water disinfection and will be traveling by vehicle, try strapping the bottles on the roof of the vehicle, exposing them to direct sunlight to help further the disinfection process.
- Bleach can be used to sanitize any object. Simply mix 1 tablespoon of bleach with 1 gallon of water. Wash and rinse objects first and then allow them to soak in bleach solution for 2 to 3 minutes. Let objects air dry.
- Rotate your bleach supply at least every 3 months in order to insure it is at full strength.
- Store at least 1 gallon of water per person per day and at least a 3-day supply of water per person.
- Store water for long-term use in the dark, since most germs require sunlight to grow.
- Seal water containers tightly and label with date filled.
- Replace stored water every six months.
- Never use a container that has contained toxic materials such as chemicals, pesticides, antifreeze or solvents for water storage.
- When retrieving water from a source, it is a good idea to place cloth or bandanna over the mouth of the bottle and let this filter large particulates out as water goes in.
- Denim, as in blue jeans, makes a good pre-filter material to run water through initially.
- When looking for groundwater, look for evergreen trees where the water is close to the surface such as cedar or willow.
- Limit your use of water for showers as much as possible and do not take baths, perhaps using no more than a gallon of water once every three days or even once a week for showering.
- Do not use the same water containers for transporting or storing potable and non-potable water.
- Rotate your potable water supply every 6 months unless it was prepared for long-term storage using a preserver.

- DO NOT drink salt water or attempt to render potable with any of the mentioned techniques.
- Always drink water when eating; it aids in digestion and will help prevent dehydration.
- Use rain barrels to collect water from any funneled water source such as storm drains, roof gutters, tin roofs, etc.
- If you have a naturally occurring water source that is at higher elevation than you are and less than 150 feet away, you can siphon the water to your location using a garden hose.
- A simple towel and bucket can be the simplest, yet effective, means of gathering water. Let towel soak up water from wet areas in yard, cracks in rocks, morning dew, etc and then wring out water into bucket.
- Instead of just quickly filling the bathtub in an emergency, use a WaterBOB (100 gallon plastic water storage bag) that fits directly in your bathtub. This way you don't have to worry about the water accidentally escaping down the drain.
- Shut off your incoming water valve if you need to stop contaminated water from entering your home.
- It is prudent to carry more than one water filtration device.
- Do not turn on the gas or electricity to your hot water heater when the tank is empty.
- Save water that you have used for washing your hands and dishes, so that it can be used for flushing toilets as well.
- Trash cans can be used to temporarily store water. Simply place several heavy-duty trash bags inside each other and place into a trash can. Then fill the inner bag with water.
- Boiled water from cooking pasta, vegetables and other foods can be retained and consumed.
- Non-lubricated condoms make good emergency water containers.
- Natural water can often be found near green vegetation by following animal tracks or by watching the movements of bees or ants.
- Old socks with no match can be cut up into cloth strips and then placed inside another sock to be used for the transpiration process.
- Drink before you are thirsty.

o All of the portable water filtration devices mentioned are excellent products. I recommend a Katadyn MyBottle and a LifeStraw in each family member's personal bugout bag. I would also highly recommend each family have at least one of the following: Katadyn pocket filter, Sawyer Complete Water Purifier System, or a LifeSaver Bottle. The LifeSaver Jerrycan per family should also be considered if you can afford it.

Do Now!

o Begin collecting old clothes or fabrics such as denim which can be used later as an excellent pre-filter for water supplies.
o Begin keeping, cleaning and removing labels from clear 2-liter soda bottles.
o Begin practicing water conservation for at least a day each week. Take a shower the way you would in a crisis situation and limit your toilet flush to one per day.
o Rotate any necessary water supplies at least every 6 months.
o Use paper plates and cups during an emergency as much as possible to conserve water and avoid the need to wash dishes.
o Learn to siphon water through a siphon hose.
o Next time it rains, experiment with ways to collect the most water.
o Save any droppers you have from used medicines, etc. Clean them good and keep to be used for dispensing chlorine or iodine for water disinfection.
o Make sure you know where the water shutoff valve is at your home.
o Teach your children not to waste water.
o Before an emergency, take a map or review computer satellite images and familiarize yourself with all natural or man-made sources of water near you such as lakes, ponds, public pools, etc. Also take note of water sources directly in your neighborhood such as small creeks, private pools and hot tubs.
o Buy at least a small supply of bottled water (3 days worth).
o Start keeping any odd socks you find in the dryer that you don't have a match for.

Checklist

Water / Filtration Items

(In no particular order)

- Coffee filters
- Liquid Clorox bleach (at least 3 gallons)(5.25% sodium hypochlorite)(not Fresh Scent or Lemon Fresh)
- Iodine solution (2% tincture)
- Dropper
- Plastic tarp
- Vitamin C tablets. (dissolvable)
- Plastic drinking straws
- Camelbak hydration system (1 per family member)
- Clear 2-liter plastic soda bottles (many)
- Water buckets (various sizes)
- Water preserver concentrate (for 55+ gallons of long-term storage)
- Rain barrels
- Garden hose (at least 3 50-foot sections)
- Cloth towels (washcloths, hand towels and full-size towels)
- Cloth strips (1 inch wide, several inches long, thick)(at least 2 dozen)
- Clear (transparent) plastic bags (at least 2 dozen)
- 55 gallon water storage barrels
- WaterBOB plastic water storage bag
- Paper towels (sturdy)
- Plastic kiddie pool (6 to 8 feet in diameter)
- Bottled water (at least 3 day supply)
- Super absorbent microfibre towel (such as ShamWow)
- Bung wrench
- Siphon/pump and hoses (for water)
- PORTABLE WATER FILTRATION/PURIFICATION DEVICE(S) (Katadyn, LifeSaver, LifeStraw, SteriPEN or Sawyer)

Ch 3 - Food / Nutrition

Even though you could probably live over three weeks without food in a survival situation, it would not be a pleasant or satisfying experience. Don't believe me? Well try going a day or two without food. As for me, a southern Cajun by background, sometimes a few hours without food is enough to put me in a state of appetite panic. Food and nutrition to your body is like gasoline to your car. You may get a little ways on fumes, but you won't get far.

The average adult male needs to eat between 2,000 and 2,700 calories a day; while the adult female should eat between 1,800 and 2,300 calories. A minimum caloric intake for survival requires between 600 to 1,000 calories per day. The following tables below give an estimate of needed calories under a non-active situation for both men and women based on various weights and ages. These are only estimates.

	Average Daily Calorie Requirement Men		
Weight (lbs)	Age 18 - 35	Age 36 - 55	Age over 55
130-165	1950-2300	1800-2150	1725-2000
165-195	2300-2650	2150-2375	2000-2250
195+	2650-2825	2375-2600	2250-2425

	Average Daily Calorie Requirement Women		
Weight (lbs)	Age 18 - 35	Age 36 - 55	Age over 55
100-130	1750-2000	1550-1800	1425-1550
130-164	2000-2250	1800-2000	1550-1675
164+	2250-2400	2000-2150	1675-1725

As stated above, these estimates were for a person who is basically inactive. For a moderately active day a person should add between 240-430 extra calories; or for a strenuously active day, add between 480-860 calories. Don't let your physical gas tank run dry. You will need the energy.

Another common question that is asked is how much food should a person store? Without going into a tremendous amount of explanation or detail, I am just going to cut to the chase. At minimum, you should have a 3-month supply stored for your group, minimum! This will get you through most short-term emergencies. Don't think that you have a 3-month supply, know for sure you do. An even better and wiser amount, if you can afford it, is to have a 6-month supply. This can be achieved by most families in a very short time period, and most homes have the ability to store this amount. This is the amount that I usually recommend to people who ask. However, if you live in a larger house in a rural community, away from the city, and most likely will be able to hunker down where you are for a while, you might want to consider extending this out to a 1-year supply. This will take some storage room and an excellent rotation plan, but you will be able to do without those grocery stores for a long time. The reason I don't recommend this much for others is simple: in a true emergency crisis in the city, chances are you will have to go mobile well before 6 months and the extra food will be difficult to transport. Gangs and looters will have already taken over and your food will end up wasted or in someone else's stomach. The city is not going to be a pretty place, folks. Sorry.

Techniques

Means of Cooking

Now that you have hunkered down or made it to a safe bugout location, your stomach has started to talk back and it is time to do some serious eating. So how are you going to cook your food? The means of cooking is as varied as any other area of survival. We just don't know what is the most appropriate in your given situation. Some means are more portable than others, some are more convenient, some are more lasting, and some are more quickly implemented. The one that you use at any particular time will depend on what you have and what you need. Here is a list of the most practical ones. I have used them all.

Open Flame - Cooking over an open flame is the most primitive means of cooking but also one of the most simplistic. All you need for this is to start a fire (discussed in a later chapter) and place your item above the heat to begin cooking. A fire pit is usually created for this on the ground by forming a circle of large rocks, if possible, wide enough to contain the fire in the center. If rocks can't be built up significantly, earth can be removed to make a literal pit in the ground which will help direct the heat and contain the fire from getting out of control. It is also advisable to place several large smooth stones at the bottom of the pit so that when heated by the fire, they will be a great source of radiant heat to more evenly cook the food. To build the fire itself, there are a couple of different methods which I will mention here. First, is the log cabin style configuration. The steps for this are as follows:

1. Place a sizable amount of tinder material in the direct center of the fire pit (preferably on top of some large, smooth stones).
2. Take multiple pieces of kindling wood roughly the same length, and begin stacking them around the tinder material to form a four-sided square.
3. Alternate placing your kindling, first front and back, then side and side, so that it resembles a log cabin (you remember lincoln logs - same thing) until you are done.
4. Once you have made a sufficient wall of kindling around the tender, place further kindling over the top, creating a roof.
5. Now light the tinder, starting the fire.
6. As the fire takes shape, and if burning well, start adding the larger pieces of firewood until you have an established fire.

The other method is the tipi style arrangement. It is very similar to the log cabin configuration except for the way the kindling is stacked. The steps for this are as follows:

1. Place a sizable amount of tinder material in the direct center of the fire pit (preferably on top of some large, smooth stones).
2. Take 4 or 5 pieces of kindling wood, roughly the same length, and stand them on their ends around the tinder material to form a tipi structure with the tops resting together. If necessary, use some twine or similar material to tie the tops together to give it stability.
3. Now begin placing the larger kindling pieces around the frame of the tipi, being careful not to collapse it.
4. Now light the tinder, starting the fire.
5. As the fire takes shape, and if burning well, start adding the larger pieces of firewood until you have an established fire.

Using either method, let the fire burn for some time until you have established a good bed of hot coals. Once you have a good, even fire bed, then cooking can begin. Dutch oven cooking is a great skill to master with the open fire pit and can make many a delicious meal. With dutch oven cooking, the cast iron oven sits directly in the coals; however, with other forms of open fire cooking, a grate or other platform should be used to keep your pots and pans above the actual flame. Also, don't ever underestimate the good, old stick with a piece of meat on the end to hold directly over the fire (marshmallows too). With this method, you can easily raise or lower the food and avoid burning.

Barrel Stove - Few items have been put to more use when cooking or grilling outdoors than the 55 gallon steel drum. In fact, a subculture has almost been created around this cooking style. I have seen steel drums simply cut in half to make two simple fire pits where they place a few large stones at the bottom, cover with tender material and kindling, then light. They add the main firewood, place a grate over the top, and they are ready to rock and roll. I have also seen where they cut them in half lengthwise, hinge them together to make a bottom and a lid, and then prepare them the same way or use charcoal. But a true barrel stove is a little more elaborate, yet still quite simple in design. It involves making a few cuts to the steel drum and installing a door, a damper, an exhaust port and a base to make a very nice, reusable stove. The actual 55 gallon steel drums can be purchased from many sources locally, but if you need my recommendation, ULine is a good source. The pieces that are needed to make a complete barrel stove are sold as kits and can be easily installed. On this I would only recommend one high quality source, and that is Vogelzang.

Fireplace/Hearth - From the time of ancient castles to the plains of the little house on the prairie, fireplace cooking has been used to provide warm food for the family. For some reason, perhaps do to our technologically advanced society, we have apparently forgotten that notion although it is still quite valid. Cooking in your home fireplace can be one of the coziest, aromatic and romantic experiences in the food preparation process. Two items that can make this experience even more enjoyable are a fireplace grill and a fireplace crane which can be used for dutch oven cooking, allowing you to swing hanging pots or kettles out over the fire. The only drawback to this method is that it is obviously not portable in any sense. But while staying put, this is a great option.

Standard Charcoal Grill - Everyone has used the basic charcoal grill either while camping, tailgating or at the park. These are simple charcoal holding basins (usually small to medium sized) which are covered with a grill and fueled by either self-lighting charcoal or a mixture of charcoal starter fluid, regular charcoal and a flame. They are usually not that durable; however, they are quite portable. For a short-term scenario these might prove fine; however, you would need to stock up on charcoal which can be extremely messy and bulky.

Propane Gas Grill - By now, most families have already invested in an outdoor propane gas grill. These tend to be larger cooking units with all the bells and whistles. While most can be moved in a pinch, they tend to not be very portable. They do however make a great first line of cooking defense for the stay at home scenario. The propane fuel source also has the advantage of being readily available and easily stored in secure bottles. As an extra benefit, this fuel can also be adapted and used for other things such as space heaters, lighting, etc. Keep in mind that when the propane runs out, so does the grill, unless you modify it to use with standard charcoal or wood after that point. They are many manufacturers of these grills but two that I highly recommend are Char-Broil and Weber.

Camping Stove - The traditional camping stove, which has almost been synonymous with the brand Coleman, is a highly portable version of the gas grill. These are usually a foot to two feet in width and, today, almost all run off of a small propane bottle. These can, however, be adapted to run off of your larger propane bottles as well which is highly convenient by allowing you to consolidate bottles between at home and travel scenarios. Another brand that makes quality stoves is Camp Chef.

Portable Mini Stove - The portable mini stove is the most portable of all the means of cooking in that it is extremely small and can be stored in your bugout bag. These stoves need to meet certain criteria. They need to be light weight, low in bulk, easy to use, durable and easy to maintain. These stoves are a basic burner which is fueled by a small canister of liquid fuel, usually a butane/propane mixture. Some mini stoves are fueled by a solid fuel block, hexamine or trioxane, such as the Esbit pocket stove. The fuel canister models that have been relied upon by mountain climbers in very harsh conditions for years include: MSR and Snow Peak.

Solar Stove - This is a totally different animal from the rest above. Solar stove cooking is an art form and needs to be practiced regularly before you can depend upon it. If you are looking for a quickly prepared meal, then this is not for you. However, if you are looking for a means that uses no other heat source other than the rays of the sun, can give you a feeling of accomplishment and self-sustainability and can provide you with some rather tasty meals when done right, then you might want to give it a try. With solar cooking, meals need to be thought out well ahead of needing them since cooking can be a 6 to 8 hour process. These stoves are somewhat portable but must be handled with a little extra care. People talk about building these themselves, but given that for most, solar cooking is iffy at best, why also introduce the problem of potentially building it wrong and ensuring total failure? This is one of those decisions where I would definitely lean toward buying it rather than building it. The Solar Oven Society has a really nice model available for purchase as well as years of experience behind them and a complete community of support to help you. A second product recommendation would be a model by Sun Oven. May the rays be with you.

Ready-Made Meals

For convenience sake, meals that are easy to make and require little energy, cooking or effort are very valuable, especially in a mobility situation. When you are trying to make it through a day and have a lot of tasks ahead of you, no one wants to spend a lot of time in the kitchen preparing a seven course meal. I am not saying you can't, or even denying that sometimes that is a great idea (to help boost morale), however as a rule, I would imagine that when push comes to shove, convenience usually wins out.

With ready-made meals you really have two types: those that are heavier, less portable, but can be absolutely critical for the long-haul, main base habitat; and those that are light, easily packable into your primary or personal bugout bags and are ideal for your short-term, portable, food and nutrition needs. Both of these have their place in proper preparations.

Bulk Foods - These are by far your heaviest and least portable of all meals. These include your basic food staples such as grains, wheat, corn, rice, flour, beans, etc. These can be stocked up on in bulk; however, they usually come in bags averaging 40 to 50 pounds each. Unless you are planning to cook for the entire town, I would advise breaking these up into smaller more preservable units, utilizing 5 gallon food grade buckets. I will go into this method later when talking about food storage; however, I wanted to mention these bulk foods here. Most of these grains, including corn and wheat, will also require milling with a grain mill. Obviously, no one would advise running through the woods carrying two, 5 gallon, 30 pound buckets in each hand and a grain mill between your teeth. Bulk food should, however, be a part of your preparedness planning. Most of these bulk items can be picked up at your local Costco or Sam's Club. The best company that I have found for these items is, by far, Honeyville, and they deliver right to your door for a very low price.

Canned Goods - These are the staple of any preppers pantry and rightfully so. Canned goods such as soups, stews, vegetables, canned meats, fruits, and one of my favorites, chili, are vital for several reasons. First, these come in several sizes, from individual servings to large #10 cans that can feed a large party. These are workable portions, and little should ever go to waste. Secondly, canned goods last for a long time, and you know what the suggested expiration date is because it is printed right on the can. This takes the guesswork out of determining whether something is fit for human consumption or not and also allows you to use this information to organize your supply for future rotation. Thirdly, they are highly stackable so that you can fit a lot of nutritional product into a very small area. This is good for obvious reasons. However, as mentioned above, these are one of the heavier ready-made meals and won't be something you are hauling with you if you only have your bugout bags as an option.

MREs - These have been the faithful companion to our soldiers in the battlefield for decades. Although they have been the butt of many a soldier's complaints, they were always a welcome sight when hunger set in after a strenuous day or encounter. With MREs, each course is packed individually inside a single overall package. These individual packages usually contain the main course, a snack, a dessert, a flavoring for a drink and some condiments, among other things. This is great because it easily allows the swapping or trading of individual pieces of the meal. I personally would often trade my spaghetti in meat sauce for my buddy's macaroni and beef or, better yet, his brownie. A 3 day supply of MREs can easily fit into an individual bugout bag. One of the main producers of MREs for civilian use is SOPAKCO.

Dehydrated Pouches - While like MREs in that they are sealed in pouches, they differ in the fact that they are usually just one individual component such as a main course, a dessert or a side dish. They are also highly convenient and are used by campers and hikers worldwide. Since they are usually not as compact as MREs, they tend to take up more space in a backpack and, therefore, fewer can be accommodated within the same space limitations. There are some off brands out there, but from my experience on this, stick with what mountain climbers and adventurers have been using for years. Some of the more trusted and well-known brands include: Mountain House, AlpineAire, Wise Food Choice and Backpacker's Pantry.

High Caloric Energy Bars or Tabs - Most people are familiar with energy bars they find in the grocery store or at the gym; however, when I am talking about an energy bar, I am talking about a single survival bar which usually contains up to 3600 calories (a complete calorie requirement for a day). Now it may not stop your stomach from rumbling, but it will save your life. These are great as part of your basic bugout bags as well since they are very small and light, taking up little room in your bag and leaving room for other necessities. They also have up to a 5 year shelf life. Two main brands that I would go with on this are: Mainstay and Datrex. Emergency survival tabs are the same concept. They are small, chewable tabs which pack a high caloric punch; however, each tab is a smaller amount of calories so you take as much as you need, when you need it. These come in two flavors: vanilla and chocolate and actually taste pretty good, while also containing all of your daily vitamin and mineral needs. These tabs are manufactured by Survival Tabs and actually have a shelf life of over 10 years, as well.

Long-Term Complete Food Providers - It is worth noting here that there are companies out there who provide 3, 6 or 12 month supplies of pre-packaged meals all as one unit. This does offer the benefit of getting quick peace of mind, without having to plan out as much or purchase over a long period of time. My caution to you is this: understand what you are getting. Make sure you understand what they are considering a single day's requirement, or you may find out that the 6 month supply may in fact only last you 5 months. Also, when stocking like this, understand that the product expiration basically occurs all at once rather than highly staggered if you had purchased things at different times. Having said all this, purchasing like this may be the best option for some people. If so, here are a couple of companies that earned mention: Wise Food Storage and Shelf Reliance.

Natural Foods

Long before we had grocery stores to purchase pre-harvested, pre-captured, pre-packaged food supplies in, our ancestors were doing it the hard way - gathering their own food from the wild. And before you even come close to running out of your purchased food supply, you should be actively pursuing a natural food supply as well. The last thing you want is to finish your last can of peas, and two weeks later you are still trying to catch that first fish or waiting for that lonely seed to sprout. There are plenty of different means to gain necessary food and nutrition in nature, and you need to be ready to take advantage of that. The following is a list of ways that you need to consider and plan for.

Hunting - That shotgun or .22 caliber rifle you got for self-defense, it has another useful purpose as well. There is a lot of game out there for the taking if need be including deer, rabbits, squirrels, bear, elk and all kinds of birds. In fact, all of your firearms are capable of taking certain types of game. Understand your ammunition and what game it is appropriate for. Two other instruments, other than firearms, which can be handy for hunting are the simple spear or throwing stick. A spear can be fashioned easily from a common broom or mop handle, or from a straight piece of tree limb or bamboo. Just sharpen one end using a knife or machete, or even attach a fish/frog gig spear tip. The throwing stick can be formed by locating or cutting a heavy piece of wood into about an arm's length piece, which is about half the thickness of your wrist. Ideally, this would be straight or boomerang shaped. Smooth the piece down so that it will be aerodynamic. With practice throwing this sidearm, you can learn to take down small to mid-size game by blunt trauma. In addition to all of this, one should remember that almost everything that flies, crawls or runs can be eaten as food if prepared properly. Sometimes the only hunting instrument you needs is your hand or a stick. But for those times you do need a firearm, the following table shows which calibers are most appropriate for common game:

	Caliber / Game Choices				
Game	12 gauge	9mm	.22	.223	Pellet
Birds	x		x		x
Squirrels	x		x		x
Rabbits	x	x	x		
Foxes	x	x	x	x	
Coyotes	x	x		x	
Goats	x	x		x	
Sheep	x			x	
Pig	x			x	
Deer	x			x	

Trapping - Trapping game means just that, using traps and snares to catch live game. Traps can be either manufactured or natural. Tomahawk Live Trap is a leading manufacturer of traps of all sizes. With a little bit of bait and one of these, dinner is right around the corner. Natural traps have two main types: the deadfall trap and tension trap. The deadfall trap is based upon the premise of a heavy object, usually a large rock, delicately propped up on one side by a series of sticks. Then when a bait, placed at the center below the rock is triggered, the rock falls and crushes the prey. The tension trap uses the idea of a stick or limb with fashioned spikes on one end which is bent and placed under tension with a trip wire that releases the tension, causing the prey to be impaled upon impact. Snares, on the other hand, form a collapsible loop that, when tightened around an animal's foot or head, creates in inescapable situation for the prey. These can be simply placed along the common paths of animals or can be spring loaded using a bent over limb to create upward tension. Although natural materials or twine can be used for the snare, I highly recommend pre-built, steel, self-locking snares from Buckshots.

Fishing - Unlike hunting or trapping, fishing is something that almost everyone has some past experience with. For this all you need is a stick, some fishing line, a hook and some bait (and some good luck, of course). Given the vast amounts of different baits and lures to choose from, you will have to stock your own tackle box to best meet your local conditions. However, when it comes to a fishing rod, I do want to recommend one heck of a small, portable, packable, sturdy little fishing rod made by Emmrod. With this you can fit an entire fishing rod, reel and tackle, directly into your primary bugout bag.

Harvesting - This is arguably the easiest ways of utilizing natural food sources. Harvesting is simply collecting and consuming food which has already grown in the wild. This can include eating fruit from trees such as apples, oranges, pears, peaches, etc. It can also include finding vegetables growing in the wild, gathering various nuts from trees or eating any of the many edible plants that exist in your environment. Some plants are poisonous; therefore, it is advisable to acquire a field guide to edible plants to make sure you can identify what you plan to consume. Some wild favorites include:

- Apples
- Rose hips
- Leeks
- Blueberries
- Cherries
- Fiddleheads
- Raspberries

- Violets
- Daylillies
- Cattails
- Blackberries
- Dandelions
- Milkweed

Growing - Gardening is the raising of your own natural food sources from seed to maturity. Gardens can range from flower box herb gardens, to raised bed square foot gardens, to full all out plowed row garden plots. Gardens can consist of vegetables, fruits, spices and herbs. The starting point for growing your own food is the acquisition of high quality heirloom seeds. It is important to get heirloom seeds rather than any genetically altered seeds so that additional seeds can be harvested from the mature plants and be used to plant future crops. One of the best sources for heirloom seeds is Heirloom Organics. Another item that can be grown indoors and be ready to consume in less than 3 days is sprouts. Sprouts are supercharged with nutrition and can be eaten with no cooking or preparation. Grow, trim, eat. You can get great information and everything you need to begin growing sprouts at Sprout People. Some of the more common edible sprouts include:

- Alfalfa
- Oats
- Clover
- Radish
- Buckwheat
- Barley
- Amaranth

Livestock - The raising and keeping of live animals, for the purpose of either consuming their output or actually consuming them directly, is something farmers and ranchers do as part of their daily lives. While this is not practical for someone who is highly mobile, if your habitat, environment and resources are suitable, this is something else to consider. Cows and goats are a good source of milk and eventually meat; and a laying hen can produce on average a single egg per day which could be a very welcome sight. Needless to say, livestock, have their own needs to drink and eat and could pose quite a burden on your own resources. Therefore, this will not be practical for most; however, it is worth mentioning.

Survival Recipes

I debated for a while whether to include this section in the book. The reasons include: this could be a book all to itself and has been on many occasions; the recipes would vary immensely depending on what you had on hand at the moment and what you were lacking; and finally, my fingers are beginning to cramp up and uh yeah. I am going to, however, include several recipes that were used to create good sources of sustenance. These include:

Jerky - This utilizes your basic meat drying techniques. The meat that is used should be lean, not fatty, or should have all visible fat trimmed prior to preparing. Wild game such as deer, elk, hog, turkey and domestic animals such as cow, lamb, rabbit, pig and goat can all make fine jerky. Here are the steps:

1. Slice your meat to 1/4 inch thick and 1 inch wide, slicing with the grain. Length can be variable and divided after drying.
2. Make up a mixture of salt, black pepper and other desired seasonings. Some seasonings could include: red pepper, powdered ginger, sesame oil, cayenne pepper, etc.) Make sure salt is included. A few drops of liquid smoke make an excellent flavor as well.
3. Coat the strips with your seasoning mixture.
4. Hang strips in the heat of the sun where predators and bugs cannot disturb it.
5. Drying times will greatly vary; however, properly dried meat should eventually turn a deep brown or burgundy color and have the texture of leather. Usually a few days will complete the process.
6. A pound of meat ends up making about 4 ounces of jerky.
7. This can be eaten by itself or added to soups and stews as well.

Pemmican - This is a very old practice that makes a life sustaining food that can keep for a very long time. To make pemmican is really easy. It starts where the previous jerky information left off. Here are the steps.

1. Take your finished jerky (for this example, 1 pound) and beat it to a pulp with a rock or other hard surface until it is ground into almost a powdery substance.
2. Take some animal fat (beef preferred) and soften it by squeezing it around in your hands. For this example, we would need about 3/4 pound of fat. (keep the fat at about 3/4 the amount of the prepared jerky)
3. Heat the fat until it is near boiling, then strain it into a pan or container. Allow to cool to a slightly warm temperature.
4. Add the powdered jerky to the fat mixture. Mix well.
5. Add some additional salt, pepper and any other dried spices that you prefer to the fat mixture, and mix well with your hands.
6. Now you can either divide the mixture into large, meatball sized portions and place on aluminum foil, or you can just form in a pan, allowing to fully cool and then cut into squares and place on aluminum foil.
7. Set in sun until it is fully dried. Pemmican can last for a very long time and is packed with energy. In fact, one can survive on it for quite a while with little else for food.

Rice Congee (Jook) - This is basically a rice-based porridge which is then spiced up with some meat and sugar or honey. It is cheap, warm and can feed a lot of people in a crisis. Here are the steps:

1. Take a large pot. Add 3 quarts of chicken stock or some other stock, if possible, and bring to a simmer. You can use just plain water if needed.
2. Add 1 cup of dried white rice to the pot and simmer for 2 to 3 hours. Stir occasionally so that nothing sticks to the bottom of the pot.
3. Now add a bit of cooked meat, some jerky or vegetables, if you have it, to the mixture.

4. Add some fresh ginger or garlic cloves, if you have it, and continue to stir occasionally until it begins to thicken.
5. This will make enough Jook for a meal for 3 to 4 people.

Bannock - This is a quick and easy fried bread to make which travels well. All you need for this recipe is some flour, baking powder, salt and water. Oh yes, you also need some lard or fat to fry it in. Here are the steps:

1. Add 3 cups of flour to a mixing bowl.
2. Add 2 teaspoons of baking powder and a pinch of salt.
3. Add some water, a little at a time, and mix well until you have a pasty dough.
4. Pinch off fist-sized balls of dough and flatten on a clean, dry surface.
5. Heat the lard up in a pan.
6. Prick the flattened dough balls many times to prepare them for frying.
7. Fry the dough patties in the lard until both sides are golden brown. Drain on a towel and enjoy plain or with jam.

Beans, Beans and Beans - What can I say about beans? Nothing, I think it says it all. So here are the steps:

1. Add 2 cups of pinto beans to a large saucepan along with 12 cups of water, a bay leaf and dried red chili peppers (if available).
2. Allow to soak overnight.
3. Bring mixture to a simmer, then add black pepper, 3 tablespoons of ground red chili peppers and 1 teaspoon of vinegar.
4. Simmer for several hours until beans are very tender, stirring often so beans do not stick to bottom. Add water if needed.
5. When beans are tender, turn off heat and add 1/2 teaspoon baking soda and 1/2 teaspoon sugar. Stir. Enjoy.

Food Storage Techniques

Now that you have decided to start storing food, the next question is how and in what? Organization is key here or you will end up wasting a lot of money and food products unnecessarily. The techniques here are very basic ones, but ones that most fail to handle properly. When it comes to storage priority here, remember: HMR - home first, mobility second, and always rotate. The first step should always be to insure that your home is adequately stocked to its maximum level utilizing normal food storage spaces (kitchen cabinets, refrigerator, freezer, pantries). Make sure that everything here can and will be eaten. If not, it is just taking up valuable space. If you are not going to eat it, don't prep it. The last thing you need is 50 cans of green beans that no one in the family likes or will eat. Always make sure the first to expire is the closest to the front so that things can be eaten in a basic order of expiration. Only once you have adequately stocked your home base, do you move on to more mobile, long-term stockpiles. The following are some basic means to food storage including where to store, as well as some techniques of how to prepare food for storage.

Cabinets and Pantries - As stated above, this should be your first line of defense. Make sure these are filled with food that you are actually willing to eat. This category includes your refrigerator and freezer as well. When the power goes off or in a short-term stay at home scenario, this is what you are going to consume first, and hopefully you won't even need to get to the other food stored away.

Rubberized Bins - Rubberized bins with lids, such as those made by Rubbermaid, make an excellent and inexpensive way to store food items, especially canned goods for future use or mobility. Put heavier items on bottom, and be sure to label each bin by writing the expiration date in permanent marker on a piece of paper or tape, placing this so that it is clearly visible on the outside of the bin. Depending on how comfortable you are with eating food past its expiration date will dictate how you divide up these bins. Some people make a bin represent a quarter of a year by labeling such as

'Q1 2012', 'Q2 2012', etc. Some are ok with using half of a year such as 'H1 2012', 'H2 2012', etc. The bins are easily stacked and will make it easy for you to know when to rotate these supplies into your consumption. The handles on the bins will also make mobility much easier and aid in the loading of bins into trucks or trailers if needed.

Mylar Bags - When dealing with large bulk items such as rice, wheat, corn, beans, etc, you will want to divide and package this up in more usable quantities and prepare for long term storage. The following technique works exceptionally well, and food stored in this fashion can last up to 25 years without any problems. For this, you will need mylar bags which can be obtained from ULine. These come in various sizes, depending on how much to you want to package together. For example, you may want to package rice in 5 pound increments but perhaps spices, such as sugar or salt, in smaller 1 pound increments. It is up to you. You will also need oxygen absorbers and a hair flat-iron. Oxygen absorbers can be obtained through Sorbent Systems in various sizes. Do not open your oxygen absorbers or expose them to air until you are ready to begin packaging. The process below works best with several people acting in an assembly line fashion. The steps are as follows:

1. Decide how much you want to place of an item in each mylar bag. Make sure you have the correct size bags necessary.
2. Pour the amount that you want into each mylar bag and stack them upright - either in a box, against the wall or some way that they will not spill over.
3. Plug in your hair flat-iron and allow to heat up.
4. The next steps need to be done in pretty rapid fashion. Have one person man the flat-iron, another hold the oxygen absorbers and a couple of others handle the bags.
5. Open the bag of oxygen absorbers.
6. Take each bag, insert an oxygen absorber, push out any extra air and flatten the remaining open end of the mylar bag.
7. Quickly clamp the flat-iron over one end of the open side of the mylar bag and run it a couple of times back and forth to seal the open end. Be careful not to get burned.

8. Once the bag is sealed tightly, set it aside. Go to next bag. Continue until finished.
9. Leave overnight until they have finished absorbing the oxygen and sealing tightly.
10. Pack finished bags into 5 gallon bucket for long-term storage.

5 Gallon Buckets - As shown above, you can place pre-packaged and sealed mylar bags into these buckets quite nicely. If they are food grade buckets with air tight seals, you can also fill them directly with bulk dry goods, toss in three 500cc oxygen absorber packets and seal them up for long-term storage as well. This, however, does not afford you the advantage of smaller quantities. Once these buckets are sealed, be sure to label them accordingly. Buckets can be obtained through ULine.

Food Rotation - IMPORTANT! Food rotation is critical to maintaining any emergency food supply. With your 5 gallon buckets that have been prepared for long-term storage, little regular attention is needed. However, with the food in your immediate cabinets and pantries, and the food stored for longer term in your rubberized bins, rotation is a must. If done correctly, most of your shopping for canned goods and emergency food items should result in you taking them directly from the car and putting them into bins rather than into your cabinets. Let the flow be from the store to your bins to your shelf, instead of from the store to the shelf to the bins. The bins which are closest to expiring should be emptied and moved to your kitchen cabinet and pantry, and new items should go directly into newly labeled bins. This way you are in a continuous food rotation system.

Some food needs to be prepared, processed or preserved before being stored. Some examples of these techniques are mentioned below; however, we are not going to go into a lot of detail on these. If you are interested in these methods, further research is advised.

Canning - This has been a staple process, especially in rural communities and farms. Canning can greatly preserve excess crops for later consumption; however, not everything can be canned safely by the home hobbyist. For this reason, consult expert documentation on the correct canning process and on what items can be safely canned at home. If canning is performed incorrectly, severe medical problems and illnesses can result. For your canning supplies, a company called Canning Pantry is a great resource.

Dehydration - Food dehydration is the process of preserving fruits, vegetables and meats (jerky) by removing the water from the item. This process can make tasty treats and allow much longer storage times. Dehydration is a process that can easily be done at home and can be engaged in by the whole family. Two of the prominent dehydrator companies I recommend are: Nesco and Excalibur.

Preserving Meat the Old Fashioned Way - Often you will have need of preserving meat, that you have killed or captured, for later use. There are four main ways of doing this. They are listed below:

○ Freezing - This is applicable if you are in a cold climate with the ability to keep things frozen for extended periods of time. Simply let the meat freeze and store it in a location that is not subject to wild predators. The meat will obviously need to be cooked once it is thawed.
○ Drying - To most effectively dry meat, cut the meat into 1/4 inch thickness and about 1 inch width with the grain (length is not really a big issue). Trim the fat. Hang the meat strips in a very sunny location that has good air flow. Once again, be sure to keep out of the reach of predators and cover, if needed, to protect from flies. Allow the meat to dry thoroughly. Properly dried meat will have a dry, crisp texture.
○ Saltwater Solution - Soaking meat in a saltwater brine solution or covering the meat with pure salt can also act as a preservative. If soaking meat, it must be totally submerged in the salt solution for about 2 weeks and then frozen or cooked and consumed within a week after removing; if covering with straight salt, it must be completely covered (all sides) and then

hung in an environment of around 60 degrees for a period of about 3 weeks. Check the meat often (every couple of days) to see if it has a rotten smell and discard if it does. Wash off the meat prior to cooking.

o Smoking - To smoke meat effectively, the meat needs to be cut to a thickness of no more than 2 inches. Create a fire using green, non-resinous hardwood. The meat needs to be suspended over the fire in some manner so no two pieces of meat touch. Do not let the fire get too hot. The idea is to smoke, not burn. Place some sort of enclosure around the fire pit to keep the smoke in. Usually, smoking overnight will make the meat last approximately 1 week, or smoking continuously for 2 days will preserve the meat for 2 to 4 weeks. If the meat has been properly smoked, it should be dark and curled and be able to be eaten without further cooking.

Tips

Basic

o With a few exceptions, you can pretty much eat anything that swims, flies, runs or crawls. So take advantage of that, and don' t let your mind get in the way of necessary survival.

o Sweet sorghum is an excellent survival crop, since it can be grown in much harsher conditions than corn and can thrive on much less water. An Amish survivalist has claimed that a person could survive on 1 tablespoon of sweet sorghum in a glass of water each day for as long as needed.

o Worms are highly edible and a great source of protein. To prepare, simply drop them into a cup of clean, potable water for a few minutes, then eat them raw.

o The average person will need at least 2000 calories per day to operate at the minimal level.

o If you stumble across a bird' s nest, take all the eggs for food except two and mark them. This way the bird will typically return to the nest and lay more eggs for the future; however, if you empty the nest, the bird will typically abandon it. Always leave the marked eggs and gather the new, unmarked ones.

- Conserve propane. Turn on only when you are ready to cook and turn off as soon as you remove food from cooking.
- Be conscious of anyone in your group that might have possible allergic reactions to certain foods.
- Always place food items in your cabinets with the first to expire nearest the front so things can be eaten in expiration order.
- Sprouts are inexpensive, quick to grow (3 days), and contain large amounts of protein, vitamins and minerals. Eat them plain or add them to other dishes.
- Even if you have spent all your reserves of propane, your outdoor gas grill can still make an excellent firebox for cooking with charcoal or other fuels. Conversion in crisis is the name of the game.
- Fish, which has been caught, should be eaten as soon as possible.
- Only prep what you are going to eat, and eat what you prep.
- Be sure to store foods for anyone with any special dietary needs.
- Stay away from mushrooms unless you know exactly which ones are not poisonous.
- A pellet gun (air rifle) can be a great means to hunt small game.
- Don't wait until all of your purchased food supplies are depleted before you start pursuing natural food sources. Pursue natural sources all along the way to supplement and make your purchased food supplies last longer.
- With just surgical tubing, duct tape and a long piece of wood or tree branch, you can make a great fishing spear.
- Store homemade jerky in glass mason jars to make it last longer.
- In an emergency, consume perishable foods first before consuming non-perishable.
- Never keep food inside a tent. Suspend it at least 10 feet off of the ground and at least 3 foot from the tree trunk. This will prevent animals such as bears from getting it.

Do Now!

○ Begin collecting all the sauce and condiment packets you can from fast food restaurants like McDonalds, Arbys, KFC and other places. Ask for extra ketchup, honey, salt and pepper, jelly packets, Arby sauce, napkins, wipes, etc.

○ Start clipping and using coupons to help stock your food preparation requirements. Savings is the name of the game.

○ Start planting a garden no matter how small. A single tomato plant in a pot can produce a lot. Plant an herb garden too.

○ Learn the art of canning and begin canning food for storage.

○ Take any inexperienced hunters out to the gun range and practice shooting some sporting clays with a shotgun. This will be good practice for shooting birds in the wild.

○ While most hunters already know how to skin and gut wild game, most city folk do not. Make sure at least one member of your party has at least a cursory knowledge of how to do this.

○ Go camping and start practicing the art of survival. Experiment with dutch oven cooking.

○ Practice hitting targets with a throwing stick. The stick should be relatively heavy and the length of your arm. Practice finding those stick and throwing them to hit targets 15 to 20 yards away.

○ Learn what is edible in the wild near you. Some plants can be poisonous and you sure don' t want to be guessing when the time comes.

○ Teach everyone basic cooking skills and cook at home more.

○ Familiarize yourself with the various hunting seasons in your area, what game is available and where public hunting lands are.

○ Set aside a day to take a complete inventory of your current home food storage areas (cabinets, refrigerator, freezer, pantries). Throw out (expired items) or donate any food items that no one in your home will eat. We all have them.

○ Make sure your propane supplies whether bottles or tanks are filled to capacity.

○ Take your kids fishing more.

○ Find several families who need to package and store away bulk items for long-term storage. Have a packaging evening to divide and seal these items into mylar bags so they can later be placed into 5 gallon buckets. This works much better with an assembly line method.

○ As a family, start identifying plants and animals, in your immediate area and your preferred bugout location, that are edible as a source of food. Think about how you would collect them and prepare them for a meal. If at all possible, start experimenting with some of these choices and plant them in your own yard.

○ If you use propane for cooking, make sure your bottles are filled. Get a few extra bottles for backup.

○ Make sure you have current hunting and fishing licenses.

○ Go camping and give dutch oven cooking a go. This can be one of the delights of any camping experience and your stomach will appreciate it too.

○ Learn the art of using snares and traps to catch wild game.

○ Begin packing non-perishable items and canned goods into rubberized bins with lids. Separate the different items into bins by the month of expiration. Tape a label to the front of the bin showing the expiration month and year. This way you can rotate items by using up the soon expiring bins and then relabeling them when you need to reuse them. Also, these can be easily loaded into a truck or trailer for transport if needed.

Checklist

Food / Nutrition Items

(In no particular order)

- Dutch oven (cast-iron)
- Griddle (cast-iron)
- Skillet (cast-iron)
- Kettle (that can withstand heat of fire or grill)
- Heirloom garden seeds (at least 1-2 acres worth)(Heirloom Organics)
- 5 gallon food buckets w/lids (ULine)
- 500cc oxygen absorbers (Sorbent Systems)
- Eating utensil set (camping style)(1 per person)
- Prepackaged meals ready to eat (MREs)(1 week supply minimum)(SOPAKCO)
- Fishing rod and reel (2 per family minimum)(1 per person preferable)(consider Emmrod, packable rod, very small and sturdy)
- Fishing tackle box w/assorted lures and supplies
- Cast net
- Energy bars (Mainstay or Datrex)
- Frog/fish gig spear tip
- Brillo cleaning steel wool pads
- Aluminum foil
- Food dehydrator (Nesco or Excalibur)
- Bulk foods (Costco, Sam' s Club or Honeyville)
- Field guide to edible plants and animals
- Hoe
- Yo-Yo automatic fishing reels (1 dozen)
- Spatula
- Strainer
- Camping stove (Coleman or Camp Chef)
- Small animal trap (Tomahawk Live Trap)
- Pellet gun (air rifle)(Gamo)
- Spoon (large for cooking)
- Whisk

- Dehydrated pouches (Mountain House, AlpineAire, Wise Food Choice or Backpacker's Pantry)
- Portable mini stove (MSR or Snow Peak)
- Vitamins and supplements
- Hand grain mill (WonderMill)
- Snare kit (steel self-locking)(assorted sizes)(Buckshots)
- Emergency survival tabs (minimum 360 tabs)(Survival Tabs)
- Chow set (stainless steel or titanium)(1 per person)
- Cook set (pot, pan and lid)(stainless steel or titanium)(non-stick)
- Esbit pocket stove w/solid fuel tablets
- Can opener (at least 2)
- Hair flat-iron/straightener
- Propane Gas Grill (Char-Broil or Weber)
- Black permanent marker
- 55 gallon steel drum (ULine)
- Barrel Stove Kit (Vogelzang)
- Mug or Cup (stainless steel or titanium)(1 per person)
- Surgical tubing (10 foot)
- Emergency can opener (1 in each person's primary bugout bag)
- Fishing line (clear)(several spools)
- Large plastic rubberized bins (to store non-perishable food)(Rubbermaid)
- Sprouts (Sprout People)
- Mylar bags (ULine)
- Baby food and formula (if needed)
- Drip irrigation tubing
- Solar stove (Solar Oven Society or Sun Oven)
- Long-term complete food packages (Wise Food Storage or Shelf Reliance)
- Pet food (at least 3 month supply)

Basic Staples Of Any Food Supply

○ Wheat
○ Flour (oat, soy, rice, wheat)
○ Canned meat
○ Salt
○ Pepper
○ Rice
○ Canned soups, stews, chili
○ Dried beans
○ Leavenings (yeast, baking soda, baking powder)
○ Salt
○ Canned vegetables
○ Honey
○ Cocoa powder
○ Oil (corn, olive, shortening)
○ Powdered Milk
○ Corn
○ Nuts and seeds
○ Instant soups
○ Peanut butter
○ Sugar (brown, white)
○ Oats
○ Bouillon cubes
○ Canned fruit
○ Instant potatoes
○ Cereals
○ Powdered eggs
○ Pasta
○ Powdered butter
○ Spices and flavorings (ketchup, mustard, salad dressings, season-all, sauces, mayonnaise)
○ Coffee and tea bags (a lot)
○ Powdered juices
○ Hard candy and gum

Ch 4 - Shelter / Habitat

Whether your situation dictates a 'hunker down' or a 'get up and go' strategy, either way, shelter and an adequate habitat must be accounted for during any survival scenario. In fact, one of the first questions we should ask ourselves when things go south is, "Where can I be safe?" and "Where can I shelter to get my thoughts together to deal with what has happened?" We rely on shelter for some of our most basic needs including health, comfort and security. It is because of this that an adequate shelter can make a bad situation much more bearable.

When it comes to health, most people are not aware that in three hours or less, environmental and situational factors could cause your core body temperature to shift into dangerous, life-threatening territories. Shelter helps protect us from adverse temperatures. From inclement weather including winds, rain and snow, it could help prevent heat stroke or hypothermia. Typically, man-made structures such as homes, buildings and emergency shelters offer better protection than outside natural shelters such as valleys, ravines and campgrounds, although this is not always true 100% of the time.

Once shelter has been established, either man-made or natural, fire is often the next step to provide both warmth and a means to cook, filter water, provide light in the darkness, etc. Man longs for a home no matter where he is. So once you have a good reliable shelter, a warm fire, a store of food and water and loved ones nearby, a place (no matter how primitive) begins to morph into a home. The decision to leave the familiarity and safety of your longtime dwelling is a highly personal one, but I trust you will know if and when that time comes. It probably will be one of the hardest decisions you will ever make, so I would never make light of it. Just remember, it is not the building that makes a home, it is life itself and the relationships of people that make a true home.

Techniques

Starting a Fire

Matches - These are an easy and well-known method of starting a fire. If matches are going to be part of your preparation supplies, they should be waterproof yet kept dry until usage. While pre-packaged waterproof or strike anywhere matches can be purchased, they tend to be costly and can be made at home. Two methods for waterproofing matches include: turpentine and candle wax. To waterproof standard, wooden matches with turpentine, simply place 2 or 3 large tablespoons of turpentine into a glass (shot glass size). Place the matches in the glass head down and allow to soak for 5 minutes. Remove the soaked matches and spread them out on a sheet of newspaper and allow to dry for 30 minutes. To waterproof matches using the candle wax method, light a large diameter candle and allow the liquid wax to accumulate below the flame. Dip the head of each match into the liquid wax and coat the entire head and up to about 1/8 of an inch of the stick. Be careful not to burn yourself with the flame or with the hot wax. Once the match is coated and starting to cool, pinch the wax around the stick to form a tight seal. Place the cooled match on some aluminum foil to completely dry. With both of these methods, the finished matches should be kept in several places and in a waterproof container, such as a small film canister along with the striking surface.

Disposable Lighters - These come in all shapes and sizes, contain a limited amount of fuel but are easily used and convenient. In a small short-term survival situation, it is hard to beat the good old-fashioned disposable lighter. Every primary and personal bugout bag should contain several of these.

Magnesium or Flint Fire Starters - For the true wilderness survivor, the magnesium or flint-based fire starters are a necessary tool. These highly surpass matches and disposable lighters in the number of strikes available and in the ability to still operate when wet. The magnesium fire starters have magnesium area where magnesium is shaved off into a small, quarter-size amount. They also have a flint area which is used to generate a spark which ignites the collected magnesium. While Coghlans makes a commercially available version of this type, the best ones can be found at local gun shows. The straight flint fire starters use a flint and striker mechanism to generate a stream of high heat intensity sparks to ignite any tinder material. The product I would recommend in this category is the Ultimate Survival Technologies BlastMatch.

Batteries and Steel Wool - Creating fire from batteries and steel wool is a rather simple process. Since we have recommended only carrying AA batteries or lithium batteries, I am going to outline the technique using two AA batteries (a cell phone battery will work also in a pinch). You must use at least two AA batteries, but three will produce even faster results. The steel wool should either be extra fine '000' or super fine '0000'. The steps for this technique are as follows:

1. Stretch the steel wool fibers out until they reach a length of six inches for two batteries or nine inches if using three batteries.
2. Place the stretched steel wool onto a flat wood surface.
3. Now gather up some flammable tinder material such as dryer lint, dry leaves, paper, etc and place it very close to the steel wool.
4. Now we need to make a battery stack. You can either form this stack in your hand by placing the batteries end to end (+ to -), holding them tightly together in the palm of your hand, or you can use a little electrical tape and hold them tightly together at the joints, making a single long battery. Either way will work.
5. Take the battery stack and push the negative end against one end of the steel wool, pinning the steel wool between the negative end of the battery stack and the wood surface below.
6. Now we are ready to light this puppy. This could get hot so be careful. Take the free end of the steel wool and hold it to the positive end of the battery stack. It should start to glow orange. Gently rub the steel wool over the positive terminal until it

starts burning.

7. Quickly take the tinder you have close by and ignite it, using the steel wool, and voila, you have fire.

Coke Can and Chocolate - Yes, you heard me right. Where in this world can you not find a discarded coke can (or similar soda can)? Not many places, and that is good for you and your survival. This is a little known technique which I have successfully performed on many occasions in order to create fire. For this process you only need 3 items: a coke can, some chocolate and a towel or cloth. The steps for this technique are as follows:

1. Find an aluminum coke can (12 oz) that is in good condition (not crumpled or misshaped). You will notice that the bottom of the can has a dull, brushed metallic look that you cannot see your reflection clearly in. We will soon change this fact. However, what makes this technique work is the parabolic shape of the bottom of the can, so do not do anything that interferes with this shape.
2. Take a piece of chocolate (a Hershey's kiss works well or a piece of a milk chocolate bar, preferably plain without nuts or any other abrasive element). I usually start with the equivalent of half of a Hershey's kiss.
3. Find a smooth piece of towel or cloth that we will use for polishing. Trim or cut a small piece of this towel or cloth off to be used as tinder later on. Begin to polish the bottom of the can by smearing the chocolate on and polishing deeply with the cloth. In a pinch, toothpaste will work as well in case you got hungry and already ate the chocolate. Put some elbow grease into it and polish deeply for 30 minutes to an hour or until you have a highly, reflective mirror surface that you can see yourself clearly in. However, the image will be distorted due to the shape of the bottom.
4. Now take a small twig (or toothpick) and place the piece of cloth you removed earlier, to be used as tinder, on the end of the twig. You can use other tinder materials as well, such as dryer lint, dry leaves, small pieces of paper, etc.

5 . Face the bottom of the can toward the sun, with you behind, so as to reflect the most light. Hold the tinder material in the center of the can bottom approximately 1 to 1 1/2 inches away from the bottom of the bowl until the heat of the sun's rays are directed at the material. Move the tender in or out to reach to optimal focal point onto the tinder.

6 . Within a short time in direct sunlight, the tinder will either ignite or begin to smolder. If smoldering, blow lightly on the tinder to blow it into flame.

Standard magnifying glass - OK! Who hasn't burned ants? As long as you have a magnifying glass and good direct sunlight, this is a tried and true method. Simply hold the magnifying glass between the direct sunlight and the tinder to be ignited. Make sure the sun is shining directly through, and the magnifying glass is 1 to 3 inches above the tinder. Adjust the magnifying glass closer or farther away until you have a single focal point of light directed onto the tinder. Hold that position. Once the tinder is smoldering, blow gently until you achieve your flame.

In order to start any fire, four things usually have to be in place: the ignition source, the tinder, the kindling and the main fuel source. The methods mentioned above will get you the ignition source, but something easily flammable needs to be there to ignite. This is referred to as the tinder. Tinder can be just about anything from dry leaves, to moss, a piece of paper, dryer lint, newspaper, cotton balls soaked in vaseline, etc. These can be purchased but just as easily found in your home or made yourself. The ignited tinder is used to catch your kindling on fire. Kindling is the small twigs and branches that will quickly begin to burn to really get the fire started. Tree bark can also make a good kindling material. Purchased fuel bars can also serve this purpose well. Finally, once the kindling is really burning, you can begin adding the main fuel source such as tree logs and thicker firewood. Before long, you have a real fire.

Sheltering Outdoors

Permanent man-made shelters such as homes, cabins, buildings, etc are easy; all the work has been done for you. But when it comes to making a shelter out in the wild, things can get a little more precarious. If you find yourself out in nature and temperatures are dropping, or night is quickly approaching, finding shelter needs to be the top priority. Apart from natural shelters, there are some portable shelters that can be constructed to provide you a temporary habitat as well. The following are some of the more common and most useful approaches:

Natural Shelters - The first step, when obvious man-made shelter is not present, is to begin looking around for natural sources of shelter which can protect you from the elements. A shallow cave can provide a highly defensible and dry shelter with only one direction needing to be secured. A fire can be built right outside the opening of the cave, giving off needed warmth and providing a means of cooking while the inside can be for sleeping. Large clumps of bushes can also be used for shelter by clearing out an area in the center and using the wall of bushes to protect you from the wind. If neither of these options are present, try looking for a tree with very low-hanging limbs or a fallen tree that you can hide beneath. Nature is all around you. Take advantage of your surroundings.

Debris Hut - When you think of a debris hut, think of a bird or animal nest. This is what you are going to build. A solid debris hut can keep you warm even when you don't have a fire or adequate clothing. The steps to construction are:

1. Find a suitable location near a large bolder or tree stump.
2. Find a long straight pole approximately two feet longer than your height. This will act as the main pole that all other poles will rest against.
3. Brace one end of your pole against the rock or tree stump and use other objects (rocks or branches) to hold it in place. This end of the pole should be at about crotch level.
4. Secure the other end of the pole to the ground, at an angle, with

heavy rocks.

5. Begin stacking smaller poles against the main pole vertically, at an angle, every few inches apart, forming a tent-like skeleton. Leave a small opening on the backside, closest the rock or stump for a small entrance.

6. Carefully climb in the structure to make sure you can fit comfortably. The tighter the fit, the better because this means added warmth. Now climb out.

7. Pile brush or small twigs on top of the shelter.

8. Now begin gathering up as much debris material as possible including dry leaves, fern branches, pine needles, grasses or moss.

9. Pile this debris on top of the brush and twigs.

10. Finally, find some more stout sticks and stack along the outside over the debris in order to prevent the wind from blowing the debris away.

Tree Pit Shelter - This type of shelter is for areas that are in deep snow. All you need for this is a tree, deep snow and your hands or a shovel. The steps to construction are:

1. Locate a large tree that has very low hanging, thick branches and has deep snow at its base.

2. Remove and keep any low hanging branches that prevent you from climbing underneath.

3. Dig down around the base of the tree until you hit bare ground or deep enough until you can fit comfortably. Remember - smaller is better.

4. Using your hand or a shovel, pack the snow tightly along the inside walls of the pit to provide stability.

5. Gather as much insulating material, such as evergreen boughs, and line the floor and interior walls with the material.

6. Take the original branches you removed from the tree, or any additional branches, and use this to cover the pit, forming the roof.

Poncho/Tarp Tent - This type of cover can actually be made from any type of windproof, waterproof material including ponchos, tarps or mylar emergency blankets. The only materials that are needed are the shelter material and some parachord or rope. The two basic designs for this shelter are the lean-to and the A-frame and are very similar. First find two trees or structures approximately 6 to 10 feet apart. Tie a length of your rope or parachord taunt between these two points at about crotch height. With the lean-to, simply attach two corners of the shelter material along the length of the rope. Then pull the other two corners taunt and secure to the ground, using sticks or rocks. With the A-frame, drape the shelter material equally over the rope hanging down. Now pull out two corners on one side, at an angle, and secure to the ground, using sticks or rocks. Do the same with the other side, creating a tent structure.

Camping Tent - The standard tent is familiar to anyone who regularly goes camping. These come in all shapes and sizes and contain all the pieces necessary to create a free standing structure. Most tents are either rated for 3 seasons or all 4 seasons. What that means is that 3 season tents are good for mild to moderate weather - usually for the fall, spring and summer. The 4 season tent is built to withstand the harsh conditions of winter and high winds. They are much sturdier tents, but both kinds have their place. There are many manufacturers of camping tents. Several that I highly recommend for quality include: Eureka, The North Face and REI.

Quick Perimeter Security

Once you have your home base established, whether that is your actual home or a temporary dwelling or campsite, perimeter security should be of concern. In a crisis situation, you very well could be faced with unexpected and uninvited guests at any hour of the day or night who may or may not be shall we say, be friendly. Unfortunately, many of those who have not read a book like this or who really just never thought they would ever have a need to get prepared for anything except breakfast at IHOP, might want to take from those who did. Sharing or not sharing is a judgment call and one that you will have to face on a per case scenario. Either way, being surprised in a crisis situation is not really what you want for your nerves. The following are ways to keep this from happening:

Sentry/Watchman - Halt, who goes there? Well, I don't think you have to worry about it being a zombie, but it very well could be a person up to no good. One of the most basic means to perimeter security is the posting of a sentry or watchman. As creepy crawlies tend to come out at night, so do a lot of human creepers; and often, all you need to do to send them scampering back into the darkness is to shine a light on the scene. This is why usually a good flashlight or spotlight is a necessity. Also acting as a sentry in rotating shifts around the clock can ensure that nothing happens unexpectedly while everyone is enjoying a nice, peaceful slumber. Make sure the sentry has a means to sounding the alarm (a whistle, horn, firearm, etc.) should a bad situation evolve.

Dog on Duty - Man's best friend can truly be man's best lifesaver. Sorry cat lovers, but don't try to convince me that Fluffy is a guard cat. At best, Fluffy is a companion and friend; at worst, in a crisis situation, Fluffy can be a burden, or on the good side, maybe lunch; but Fluffy is not going to be a security help. A good guard dog, on the other hand, can be worth its weight in gold during an emergency. When I say a good guard dog, I need to clarify. A dog by itself is ok; a dog that barks at its own tail or continuously is better; but a truly trained guard dog that barks at legitimate threats, stays quiet at other times and obeys your commands is the best, by far. A good guard dog can be chained to an area and used to warn you in the event of a potential upcoming threat. Prize these animals. And cat lovers, don't send me mail. I was just kidding, maybe.

Warning Signs - Do you know what a good can of spray paint can do for you? A lot. Some people just need to know that a location is occupied before they turn the other way. You need to think about your situation when the time comes and evaluate which signs will keep people away. For example, if the scenario is a pandemic, signs that read 'Contaminated Stay Away' might be the best choice. At other times a good 'Keep Out' or 'Do Not Enter' sign might do the trick. When out in nature and needing to keep people away, make sure you place signs in a location that will be seen way before they see you. It does no good if you post a 'Virus Here' sign right next to your camp where they see people singing Kumbaya and dancing merrily. Use your head and common sense. There may also be times when you want people to think your home is a non-value target and that they would be wasting their time to enter. In this case, perhaps you should throw a few broken items out in the yard and spray paint 'Nothing Left' in graffiti style letters across your garage door. Every situation can be different. Some examples of some signs that could help in your situation include:

- Keep Out
- Trespassers Will Be Shot
- Do Not Enter
- Contaminated Stay Away
- No Trespassing
- Looted
- 3 Dead
- Nothing Left
- Virus Here
- Will Shoot
- Private Property Will Defend

Line, Bells and Cans - Short of placing land mines around your area, there are certain improvised perimeter security warning systems that can be constructed quite easily and yet be highly effective. One of these involves some simple fishing line, some Christmas jingle bells and a few empty aluminum soda cans. First, just enlarge the opening on the top of the can so that a couple of jingle bells can be dropped inside. Now poke a couple of holes on the opposite sides of the can right below the top (a nail works good for this). Simply string the fishing line through the holes in the can sides, and then string the line around the perimeter that you want to guard. Keep it taunt, and make sure the line is approximately shin high off the ground. Make sure the cans are near the bases of trees so that they are not in the direct paths most likely followed. These may possibly be seen during the day, but at night they will be virtually invisible. When an intruder approaches and trips the line, the bells will jingle loudly, warning you of his approach. Easy, yet effective.

Tips
Basic

- Storing old phonebooks and catalogs for usage as toilet paper is a lot more space effective than stocking large quantities of actual toilet paper. Pages out of phonebooks and catalogs, once crumpled several times, become quite soft and usable.
- Always keep dry and sheltered, and start a fire before you need it.
- Conceal most of your preparation activities by utilizing your backyard concealment and garage areas. You don't want to advertise that you are the best prepared house in the neighborhood.
- To prevent flooding of your tent, dig a channel around the base of your tent and leading downhill.
- Without electricity, most garage doors are very heavy to lift. Make sure you can lift the garage door in a situation like this and have something sturdy to prop under it to keep it open in order to get out necessary vehicles, trailers, etc.
- It is prudent to carry more than one fire making tool.
- Toilet paper will compact and store much more efficiently if you take the cardboard tube out and smash it flat.
- Straw, dry pine needles, wood shavings and dead grass make good fire tinder materials. Cardboard, small twigs and split wood make excellent kindling materials to use with your tinder.
- After each use of your sleeping bag, turn it inside out and let it air dry, preferably in the sun.
- Caught without electricity in your home, you can improve insulation by stuffing towels, rags and papers in cracks around doors and windows. Also, seal off all rooms, other than the room that has the heat source.
- Should you ever need to seal your house off against fallout or contamination, use 6 mil plastic sheeting and duct tape to seal

off any doors and windows to the outside. Also, make sure you shut off any ventilation systems.

○ In order to elevate your sleeping bag above wet or soggy ground, you can make a raised floor of logs and place the sleeping bag on that.

○ DEET insect repellent should not be applied over cuts, wounds or irritated skin. It should also not be applied directly to the face but rather sprayed onto the hands and then rubbed onto the face.

○ You can estimate how many miles an approaching storm is away, by counting the seconds between the lightning and thunder and dividing by 5.

○ In case of a house fire, remember the basics: don't open doors that are hot to touch, if smoky stay low and if clothing catches fire then stop, drop and roll. Also, get out as quickly and safely as possible. Once out, do not go back in.

○ Plant materials such as leaves, corn husks and banana peels can be used as a toilet paper substitute.

○ Organize a sentry in rotating shifts, so that a person is awake around the clock to provide a security watch.

○ Never let your sleeping bags get wet. Always keep them inside a waterproof cover or sack. If they do get wet, dry them in the air or sun as soon as possible.

○ Listerine, when put into a spray bottle and sprayed around an area, makes a good mosquito repellent.

○ There may be a time when spray painting a warning on your house or habitat may be appropriate to keep unwanted visitors from desiring to enter. For example, in a mass pandemic situation, spray painting 'Infected', 'Contaminated' or 'Danger Keep Out' may do the trick.

○ Carry a small non-electric pencil sharpener in your bugout bag. You can use this to make shavings from small twigs which can be used as tinder to start a fire.

○ When camping outdoors at night, always keep a pee bottle with you so you don't have to leave the tent in the middle of the night unnecessarily when nature calls. This bottle should be labeled as such and only used for that. It should have a screw on lid and you hopefully should have good aim.

○ When caught outside and you need to shelter yourself from a potential blast, crouching behind walls or fallen trees makes fair protection, lying in ditches or ravines is better protection, and hiding inside caves or concrete/steel culverts affords the best protection. If in urban environment, seek steel and reinforced concrete buildings, and move to the basement level if possible.

○ A disposable lighter or magnesium fire starter should be carried on your person at all times.

○ You should be thinking about and doing recon for a potential campsite at least 3 hours prior to dusk, and you should be actively preparing a campsite no less than 2 hours before dusk.

Do Now!

○ Always pick up those free newspapers (Thrifty Nickel, Penny Saver, etc.) outside businesses, especially right before they replace them with newer ones. These can be used for fire starting, toilet paper, insulation and a host of other uses.

○ Save old phonebooks and catalogs (especially thick ones).

○ Begin collecting the lint from your dryer and pack it into zip lock bags. This makes excellent fire starting material.

○ Start collecting as much firewood as possible and store it in a place where it is not readily visible.

○ Make sure at least one responsible party knows how to turn off the water, electricity and gas at the main switch.

○ If you already have a bugout location, such as a second home in the country, begin moving and storing your supplies there now. However, at least keep your basic family bugout bags with you at all times so that you will be prepared until you can reach that location.

○ Make your own fire starter balls. It is easy and works incredibly well. Simply heat some vaseline petroleum jelly in the oven (or microwave) in a bowl. Do not overheat, as it can get very hot and burn you. Now simply saturate each cotton ball in the melted vaseline, and place the soaked balls on a piece of wax paper to cool. Once cooled, stuff as many as you can into a zip lock bag for storage. Each ball, when lit, will burn for a very long time and make an excellent fire starter. They are cheap, so make a lot.

○ Make sure your home has a backflow prevention valve on the sewer line into your house to prevent waste and other sewage from flowing into your house during a flood or other sewer problem.

○ Start clearing out things around your home to free up space for necessary supplies. This could mean holding a garage sale, or donating a lot of stuff to Goodwill. Remember to write them down for a tax deduction.

○ Shut off your power for a weekend, and note any problems which you encounter. Then plan for these accordingly.

○ Send your dog to obedience school and train him on some useful skills.

○ Keep any Christmas jingle bells that you receive on any presents or gifts.

○ Begin getting rid of things around the house that serve no purpose and are just taking up needed storage space. Cash as much of them in as you can and use that money to buy needed supplies.

○ Practice lifting and securing the garage door should there be no power or electricity.

○ Locate natural areas around your home, or buildings nearby, that would serve as a good shelter location from a strong blast.

○ Always carry a lighter (or matches) with you at all times, along with some materials for tinder (paper, lint, etc.)

○ Organize the storage spaces you have. Organization is key to finding things and making the most efficient use of the space.

Checklist

Shelter / Habitat Items

(In no particular order)

- 550 Parachord (500 yards)
- Can of flat, black spray paint
- Space emergency blanket (1 per person)
- Emergency sleeping bag (1 per person)
- Sleeping bags (0 or below degree rating)(1 per person)(Eureka, The North Face or Marmot)
- Bucket toilet lid
- Large family tent (3 or 4 season tent)(Eureka, The North Face or REI)
- Waterproof fire sticks
- Sanitary waste bags
- Smaller tent (2-3 person tent which can fit in the backpack)(Eureka, The North Face or REI)
- Emergency candles
- Fishing line (clear 12 lb)(several spools)
- Inflatable pillow (1 per person)
- Holiday jingle bells (at least a dozen)
- Crank lantern(s)
- Portable ice chest (both large and small)
- Plastic sheeting (6 mil)(enough to cover every door and window in the house, plus a little extra)
- Cot (1 per person)
- Folding chairs (camping style)(good quality)
- Toilet paper (at least a 1 week supply)
- Waterproof matches
- Pencil sharpener (small and non-electric)
- Portable generator (Generac or Troy-Bilt)
- Bag of chocolate chips
- Dog chain and tie down (50 foot)(if appropriate)
- Field hatchet (Timberline or Gerber)
- Trioxane fuel bars
- Shovel/entrenching tool

- DEET insect repellent
- BlastMatch (Ultimate Survival Technologies)
- Disposable lighters (several)
- Sleeping pad (1 per person)(Therm-a-Rest)
- Wetfire fire starting tinder
- Magnesium fire starter (Coghlans)
- Mosquito netting
- Portable indoor space heater (propane or natural gas)(ProCom or Mr. Heater)
- Steel wool pads (no soaps or detergents)(extra fine '000' or super fine '0000' steel wool)
- Home repair Needles (assorted sizes)
- 55 gallon steel drum
- Lamp oil
- Wood splitting axe
- SaberCut survival hand saw (Ultimate Survival Technologies)
- Cotton balls
- Vaseline petroleum jelly
- Wool blankets (at least 2 for each person)

Ch 5 - Medical / First Aid

Wow, this is a broad topic. Libraries have been written on rendering medical care and first aid techniques. Now obviously, I don't have the time, qualifications or expertise to play doctor (at least not in the occupational sense); therefore, the following chapter is just a basic common sense guide and should be taken as such. One of the first things you should do in this area is to go out and purchase a detailed and complete first aid manual. I like to keep a comprehensive, first aid manual in my supplies but also a pocket, basic first aid manual in my primary bugout bag. This way I can easily handle quick medical emergencies but have much more detailed information to follow up with and research completely. Any further questions you might have should be directed to a licensed medical professional.

I am going to divide this medical/first aid chapter up into three sections, two of which I will address and one that I will not. The area that I will not address is your current or future prescription medications that you are taking currently or will potentially be taking in the days ahead. I am assuming that these were prescribed to you by your physician and all instructions regarding such are just that - between you and your physician. I am making no claim to act as your physician in any way. The bottom line is: I am not your doctor, and you should consult your physician whenever possible! Now that I have made that perfectly clear, the two areas that I will discuss are: some very basic first aid techniques and some well-known natural remedies that have been used in the past.

Also, I will say this: spend time working on your first aid kit. You can have all the food, shelter and water you need; but if you are hurt or face a life-threatening illness and don't have what you need, then what was it all for? You need to take care of yourself and your family. In your supplies you should have your main first aid kit which is loaded out, but you should also have several smaller mini first aid kits in places, like in your vehicle and in each person's personal bugout bag. At the minimum, these should be able to treat minor cuts, burns and scrapes. A well thought out first aid kit will help protect your family for many years to come.

Techniques

Basic, Basic First Aid

Basic Resuscitation - If you come across a person who has collapsed or is totally unresponsive, here are the steps for basic resuscitation. If you are not comfortable with performing emergency breathing, then just do chest compressions when needed. It is always better than doing nothing at all.

1. Call, or have someone call 911 if possible.
2. Place two fingers under the person's chin and a hand on their forehead. Tilt their head back to open their airway. Check for and remove any obstructions.
3. Listen and feel for signs of breathing. If they are breathing, turn them on their side and seek help. If they are not breathing, continue on.
4. Pinch off their nose, clamp your mouth over their mouth and blow steadily for two seconds or until their chest rises. Remove mouth and let chest collapse. Repeat one more time.
5. Check for circulation by feeling for a pulse on the side of their windpipe. If there is no pulse, continue on.
6. Place the heel of your hand, two finger widths up, from the end of the breastbone and place your other hand on top of the first. Press down firmly, about 2 inches, and then release.
7. Perform 30 repetitions of this chest compression at a rate faster than 1 per second.
8. Repeat this process of 2 breaths and then 30 chest compressions until they begin breathing on their own or until help arrives.

Shock - Lay the person down on a sleeping bag, coat or other soft surface. Raise their feet higher than their head. Loosen all restrictive clothing and cover them with a sleeping bag, coat or other soft warm material. Seek medical attention.

Poisoning - If poisoning is from contact on skin, remove any contaminated clothing. Wash off thoroughly with water and then remove residue by wiping with alcohol preps. If poisoning was internal and the person is breathing but unconscious, place them on their side with one knee bent. Seek medical attention.

Cramps - To relieve a cramp in the leg or knee, raise the leg in the air and massage the muscles until they relax. If the cramp is in the foot, gently massage the ball of the foot and stretch the toes until relieved. Make sure they receive adequate fluid and electrolytes. Seek medical attention.

Blisters - It is better not to burst a blister; however, if you must, first clean the area with an alcohol prep. Sterilize a needle and let it cool. Slide it into the edge of the blister, parallel to the skin surface. Carefully apply pressure to the blister from the side until the fluid has been removed. Cover the blister with a clean dressing or moleskin. Seek medical attention.

Animal Bite - Pour water over the wound for at least 5 minutes. Cover the wound with a sterile dressing. If the wound was bleeding, apply direct pressure with a gauze pad and raise the area above the heart. Then apply bandage. Seek medical attention.

Snake Bite - Do not panic! Wash the wound thoroughly but quickly. Apply direct pressure to the bite wound. Bandage the area firmly above and below the wound to isolate the venom. Do not attempt to suck out the venom, apply a tourniquet or cut the wound. Seek medical attention.

Stings and Ticks - With insect stings, carefully remove the stinger with tweezers, being careful not to squeeze the poison sac. If the sting was from a marine animal, wash the area with vinegar and then remove the stingers. For ticks, either coat the tick with vaseline or dab with insect repellent until it loosens its grip. Then remove it carefully with tweezers. Seek medical attention.

External Bleeding - Lie the victim down. Raise their bleeding limb and apply pressure on the wound with a gauze pad until the bleeding stops. Apply a sterile dressing to the wounded area, then bandage the wound firmly, but do not cut off circulation.

You can test the circulation by gently pressing a fingernail for an arm wound, or a toenail for a leg/foot wound. If the color does not return quickly, re-bandage more loosely. Seek medical attention.

Burns - Immerse the would immediately in cold water and allow it to stay there until the skin has cooled. Cover the wound with a clean dressing. Lightly bandage the area. Do not put any ointment on the burn. Seek medical attention.

Dehydration - Move the person to a cool place and give them plenty of food and electrolyte solutions. Elevate their feet to ease the blood flow to vital areas. If you do not have ready-made electrolyte solution, you can maintain their fluid level by taking one teaspoon of salt and one teaspoon of sugar and mixing them into one quart of water. Have the person drink slowly. Seek medical attention.

Heatstroke - Quickly place the person in the shade. If a cool indoor shelter is not available, soak a sleeping bag liner or towel in cool water and place over their body below the head. Fan the person's face to help them cool down. Do not immerse them directly in cold water. Seek medical attention.

Broken Bones - The main task with a broken limb is to immobilize it, using a splint until medical attention can be given. To do this, find a solid straight stick, a piece of bark or other object of the length that is needed. Place a towel or other padding around the limb and then place the splint firmly against it. Secure the splint to the limb, using any type of cordage available, but do not cut off circulation. Seek medical attention.

Choking - Several methods can be used to alleviate choking. First, you can sit the person down, with their head lower than their chest. Slap them firmly between the shoulder blades five times. Another method is the abdominal thrust. Stand behind the person, interlock your hands below their ribcage and sharply pull upwards. If it is a child who is choking, do not use abdominal thrusts. Instead, bend the child over your knee and strike them between the shoulder blades with the heel of your hand. Seek medical attention.

Nosebleeds - Sit the person down with their head leaning forward slightly. Pinch the bridge of their nose until the bleeding stops. Some ice (if available) wrapped in a thin cloth, can also be applied to the area to help the bleeding stop. Seed medical attention.

NOTE: These are just general guidelines and in no way should be used in lieu of a technical first-aid manual and in seeking immediate medical help. Professional medical help should be sought as quickly as possible.

Natural Remedies

Do you realize there was a time before doctors and giant pharmaceutical houses, which pop out hundreds of thousands of pills an hour trying to create their prescription monopolies and reap huge profits off of the dependencies of their patients? Do you also realize there was a time when most people gathered and prepared their own remedies for medical conditions? I know it is hard to fathom, but yes, it is true. And it wasn't that long ago.

Man-made synthetic medications have reached staggering proportions in the past century. While many are incredibly beneficial and are lifesaving drugs which are necessary to treat complicated illnesses, most offer unwanted side effects or simply mask underlying problems. Some, in fact, create situations which are worse than if there were never medications taken at all. One thing is clear: they have taken the focus off of what our Maker has provided naturally to assist in dealing with various conditions. Some of these natural remedies are listed below:

Cayenne Red Pepper (Capsicum Annuum) - Acts as a powerful pain reliever when applied topically, helps to stop bleeding and heal wounds, treats osteoarthritis and shingles and eases seasickness and fevers.

Milk Thistle (Silybum Adans) - Used to treat liver disorders and increase liver function. Also aids in lessening the damage to the liver due to mushroom poisoning.

Black Cohosh (Actaea Racemosa) - Relieves menstrual cramps, mood swings, calms nerves and relieves symptoms of menopause.

Fennel (Foeniculum Vulgare) - Treats hernia, indigestion and abdominal pain. Can be brewed in tea to alleviate a chronic cough and act as an expectorant to help clear mucus from the lungs.

Rosemary (Rosmarinus Officinalis) - Treats muscle pain, indigestion, arthritis and improves circulation. Can be brewed into a tea.

Valerian (Valarian Officinalis) - Used to treat insomnia, nervousness, anxiety, seizures and epilepsy. Can also be used to treat headaches and migraines.

Catnip (Nepeta Cataria) - Aids in digestion, acts as a natural sedative and eases colic and diarrhea. Can be brewed into a tea to help treat dehydration, diarrhea and high body temperatures.

Purple Coneflower (Echinacea Purpurea) - Used to treat infections, wounds, malaria, diphtheria and blood poisoning. Brewed into a tea, it helps the body regain strength and heal more quickly. Helps to rid the body of the common cold three times faster than doing nothing.

Chamomile (Anthemis Nobilis) - Has a calming power and soothing effect when brewed into a tea. Also helps to prevent nightmares and relieves stress, including anxiety and panic attacks.

Feverfew (Tanacetum Parthenium) - Relieves pain from migraines, relieves muscle spasms and prevents constriction of blood vessels in the brain.

Marshmallow (Althaea Officinalis) - Used to treat bronchitis, asthma, cough, sore throat and even the common cold. Can help to dissolve kidney stone and improve kidney function.

Comfrey (Symphytum Officinale) - Used to treat external wounds and reduce inflammation caused by sprains and broken bones. Used to create external salves and poultices.

Evening Primrose (Oenothera Biennis) - Used to treat eczema, dermatitis and skin allergies. Also helps to strengthen liver function, alleviate symptoms of nerve disorders, reduce inflammation and ease bloating of menstrual discomfort.

Chicory Root (Cichorium Intybus) - Can be added to coffee and is a natural sedative and anti-inflammatory. Can treat jaundice and high cholesterol. Helps to heal wounds, resist gall stones and is useful in helping the body rid itself of parasites.

Lavender (Lavandula Officinalis) - Natural remedy for insomnia, depression and anxiety. Known for its soothing effect.

Boneset (Eupatorium Perfoliatum) - Treats symptoms of influenza, helps detoxify the body by removing excess uric acid, removes other body toxins and treats aches, pains and fever.

Arnica (Arnica Montana) - Can be used as a cream or ointment to reduce inflammation, sooth muscles and heal wounds. Brewed as a tea to relieve stress and emotional trauma.

Calendula (Calendula Officinalis) - Treats upset stomach and ulcers and relieves menstrual cramps. Acts as an anti-inflammatory, antiviral and antibacterial. Makes a good poultice to help heal wounds.

Hyssop (Hyssopus Officinalis) - Acts as an expectorant and stimulant. Relieves muscle aches and bruises. When brewed in a tea, it aids with breathing problems and can be helpful to asthmatics.

Yarrow (Achillea Millefolium) - Can be used to stop bleeding and treat inflammation, fever and infection. Can be used topically to ease the discomfort of hemorrhoids. When brewed in a tea, it can be used to help stop diarrhea and fight against bacterial infections.

Lemon Balm (Melissa Officinalis) - Used to help treat sleep disorders when brewed as a tea. Acts as a natural mosquito repellent.

Disclaimer: Please consult with your physician, pharmacist or health care provider before taking any home remedies. Only they can provide you with advice on what is safe and effective for your unique needs or medical history.

Tips

Basic

- If your body is severely lacking in electrolytes, add 1/4 teaspoon of salt to 1 liter of water and drink to help regain balance.
- A teaspoon of salt mixed with a cup of water can act as a mouthwash substitute.
- In a survival situation, never drink seawater, blood, alcoholic beverages or urine.
- Personal hygiene is very important to health. If you are short on water, take some soapy water and a washcloth and wash areas that are prone to infection including feet, crotch, hands, armpits and hair.
- Raw apple cider vinegar has an immense amount of uses. Look it up.
- Keep your fingernails short, trimming regularly.
- Wear clean socks and underwear each day.
- Remove a tick by covering it with vaseline, thereby cutting off its air supply. It will let go and can be removed completely.
- Unless there is imminent danger, do not attempt to move victims until you have discovered what is wrong with them.

- If exposed to a radiation threat, take potassium iodide for up to 10 days and remove yourself from the contaminated area.
- Some animal antibiotics will work just fine on humans, given the right dosage. These can be bought easily, in bulk, from a vet supply without the need for a doctor' s prescription. Do your own research on this.
- Meat tenderizer is good to treat bee stings.
- Baking soda, baby powder or cornstarch can be a deodorant substitute.
- Treat any cuts, scrapes or blisters immediately to avoid possible infections.
- Ginger tea works very well for treating nausea.
- Super glue can be used to make emergency sutures.
- Baking soda and water can be used as a toothpaste substitute.
- If you feel you have been exposed to any radioactive, chemical or biological contamination, remove and discard all outer clothing, and quickly wash all exposed skin and hair with soap and water. A bleach/water solution (1 part bleach to 9 parts water) can also be used on contaminated skin surfaces.
- Many hazards to your health come by potential inhalation. If you have nothing else, wet a paper towel, rag or bandanna and use this to cover your nose and mouth, while also shielding your eyes.

Do Now!

- Learn basic first aid including CPR. This should be done by every adult/teenager in the group.
- Make sure everyone, especially children, are up-to-date on immunizations.
- Complete any necessary dental work.
- Start exercising as a family. Getting in the best physical shape possible should be a top priority.
- Grow a medicinal plant garden, and learn about the uses of each plant.
- Take pride in building a robust, primary first aid kit for the family or group.

- Raw apple cider vinegar. Learn about it. Drink it. Love it.
- Go ahead and purchase all refills of any long-term needed medications.

Checklist

Medical / First Aid Items

(In no particular order)

- Disposable baby wipes
- Liquid anti-bacterial soap/hand wash (60% or more alcohol)
- Eucalyptus 100% pure essential oil
- Lavender oil
- Chewable Pepto-Bismol tablets
- Burn cream
- Lip ointment (Blistex or Carmex)
- Safety pins (various sizes)
- Alcohol prep pads
- Gauze sponges (2″ X 2″, 4″ X 4″)
- First aid box (fishing tackle box style)(large)
- Bandages (3/8″ X 1″)
- Bandages (3/4″ X 3″)
- Antiseptic towelettes
- N95 or N100 respiratory masks (10 per person minimum)
- Knee brace
- Arm sling
- Abdominal pad (8″ X 10″)
- Eye patch
- Moleskin
- Sterile bandage roll (4.5″ X 144″)
- Skin closure strips (1/4″ X 4″)
- Waterproof tape (1/2″ X 10 yards)
- Imodium tablets
- Antacids (Tums or Rolaids)
- Ipecac syrup (1 oz)
- Ammonia capsules
- Eye drops (Visine)
- Ace bandages (3″)
- Ace bandages (4″)
- Rubber tubing
- Sterile pads (2″ X 3″, 4″ X 4″)

- Tongue depressors
- Benzoin swabs
- Glucose tablets
- Isopropyl alcohol
- Bandage scissors
- Bandaids w/antibiotic (assorted sizes)
- Disposable gloves
- Aloe vera gel
- Listerine
- Tweezers
- KI4U potassium iodide (bottle of 200 minimum)
- Tylenol extra strength (Acetaminophen)
- Motrin fever reliever
- QR blood stopper
- Butterfly closures
- Tamiflu (1 10-capsule treatment per person)
- Sunscreen (Bullfrog Surfer Formula Gel)
- Army foot powder
- Triangular bandage
- Stethoscope
- 30cc irrigation syringe
- Blood pressure cuff
- Thermometer (if battery, AA only)
- Neosporin plus pain relief
- Benadryl allergy antihistamine
- Sudafed decongestant
- Eyewash bottle (4 oz)
- Lotrimin antifungal cream
- Simply Sleep tablets
- Heat pack
- Cold pack
- Snake bite kit
- Dental floss
- Raw apple cider vinegar
- Pocket first aid manual (basics and concise)
- First aid manual (extensive and detailed)
- Surgical tape
- Terramycin-343 antibiotics

- Hydrocortisone cream
- Cotton swabs (QTip)
- Telfa adhesive pads
- Magnifier
- Super glue
- Scalpel
- Surgical/sutures kit
- EpiPen (to treat severe allergic reactions)
- Adequate supplies of all needed prescription medications
- Throat lozenges

Ch 6 - Communications / Navigation / Signaling

Communications, navigation and signaling (comm/nav/sig or CNS) are the next important topics to be discussed in this book. Now that you find yourself in no present danger (from threats or medical conditions), have adequate water and food and have made use of available shelter, what's next? Generally, this means either making contact with others in your group or the outside world, getting from point A to point B or getting rescued.

Communications is the means by which you will be able to keep in touch with other members of your party, as well as contact others outside your group. This is vitally important for obvious reasons. Although losing touch with the outside world has a romantic appeal, being in the information black hole can lead to many unforeseen dangers and cause you to miss valuable opportunities. In today's world, the ability to communicate is not even given a second thought. Just about everyone over the age of 12 has a cell phone, access to computers, and a facebook or skype account. Access and instant communication are only seconds away. That could change rapidly.

Navigation is the means by which you will be able to get to a desired destination. Not only is it a means to find your way to something, but sometimes, more importantly, it is a means to find your way back. In the good ole days, people were lucky to have a map that you would unfold into an unwieldy mass of grid lines and location listings. Then came a decent highway system where the average road traveler could rely on highway signs and convenience stores. Today, most cars are equipped with GPS guidance that would have changed the whole fate of the early explorers and maybe helped them find that lost city of gold. With this, it is almost impossible to get lost, almost. The bottom line is that we are navigationally spoiled beyond belief.

Finally, signaling is the means to get someone's attention, plain and simple; whether that be someone in your own group, or a rescue party looking for you, or a stray individual who you need to let know that you are in trouble. Signaling can take many forms from fire to smoke to flares to leaving a sign using rocks. Whatever will let someone know where you are can be a useful signal.

All three areas of CNS are equally important to survival, or in relation to any emergency situation. So don't neglect these areas, or you may simply find yourself, well, lost!

Techniques

Lines of Communication

One of the first fatalities in most emergency situations is the communication system. It doesn't take much to disrupt phone lines or cell phone towers, and all of a sudden you find yourself with no easy way to communicate to family or friends. It is amazing and scary how dependent we have all become on these convenient means of communication. Not only that, but even if these means are still operational, everyone trying to communicate at the same time often puts these systems into an overload status, and you could spends hours or days trying to get through. As the old adage says, "Don't put all your eggs into one basket," and we shouldn't either when it comes to communication methods. Situations can cause any of these methods to be the best choice at that particular time.

Standard Phone Lines - Installed in most homes and nearly all businesses, the standard hardwired phone lines are usually the first communication means to try, provided they are in service. Many disasters will take out these lines very quickly due to downed telephone poles, cut cables or lightning strikes.

Cell Phones - In today's world, just about everyone has one. Cell phones are incredibly mobile and useful, as long as the service is up and the towers are working. You can dial 911 from just about anywhere and communications with family or persons in your party can be easily handled. These could be difficult to use in highly mountainous or rural areas where coverage is not existent. Everyone should at least have a prepaid cell phone in their primary bugout bag for emergency use.

2-Way Handheld Radios - Most of us were familiar with these radios from a very early age when we played army as a child. Although the name has gotten a little more professional sounding, they are still the basic walkie-talkies. Whereas in the old days, these devices were paired together on a single frequency, today they can be used in unlimited numbers since they are capable of tuning in to a whole range of available channels. The two manufacturers that I highly recommend in this area are Midland and Motorola. Most of these radios have a range of anywhere from 16 to 28 miles, and a few even go beyond that by utilizing a repeater service. Generally, these radios also come with the added benefit of receiving the NOAA weather channels as well as keeping up with weather related emergencies.

CB Radios - Breaker, breaker good buddy! While still in use by most truckers today, most of us remember CB radios from the good old days when Smokey the Bandit was on the big screen and everyone had to have one. That didn't last long. CB radios did and still have good potential for emergency communications in a disaster, though most of these radios come with the ability to pick up all 40 of the citizen's band channels as well as have NOAA weather channels for weather monitoring. The main limitation to the CB radio is range, which is limited to about a 5 mile maximum. However, if near a highway, CB radios can pick up a wealth of information and make contact with others as well. The two recommended brands in this area are Midland and Cobra.

Emergency Scanners - These are sometimes referred to as police scanners, although they scan various local frequencies and pick up everything from police to fire department to air traffic and other local transmissions which are taking place around you. These quickly scan automatically through multitudes of frequencies and stop when they detect active transmissions. Emergency scanners are very valuable tools in a disaster since they allow you to hear what is going on with emergency personnel around you. When it comes to portable emergency scanners, one name always comes to mind and that is Uniden.

HAM Radio/Transmitters - Now we are getting into the big boys. When it comes to long-distance two-way communication in a grid down situation, HAM radio is the way to go. These radios can transmit over vast distances and literally around the globe. An estimated 2 million people are regularly involved with HAM (amateur) radio across the world. In order to use HAM radio, you must be licensed and show a basic understanding of HAM terminology and key concepts of radio equipment. Once you are licensed, you are given an identifying call sign to be used in all your broadcasts. Entry into this world of amateur radio can be affordable but can quickly spiral into a costly but valuable endeavor with larger and more powerful equipment. There are multiple manufacturers in this space; however, some of the preferred ones include Yaesu, Kenwood, Icom and Alinco.

Shortwave Radios - With these you cannot transmit, but you can listen to broadcasts from around the world. They usually pick up AM/FM stations, NOAA weather stations as well as the shortwave bands across the globe. At least one shortwave radio is a must so that you can keep informed about any multi-national situation going on. These are small and highly portable and come in battery operated or crank models. The crank models are highly preferred since you can run them on batteries or on simple muscle power whenever needed. The shortwave radio that is highly suggested is the Eton which is currently used by the American Red Cross.

Navigating in a Pinch

Finding your way down the highway is an easy task in today's automobiles. We have built-in GPS navigation, signage every few miles and, at every exit, gas stations and convenience stores everywhere you look. Get lost, no problem, just stop and ask someone. Now take those same people and drop them in the middle of the woods and watch them panic. Even basic navigation skills are totally foreign to most travelers today. The basic skill of getting from here to there is a must in any type of survival situation, and there are many things that can help in this task.

Maps - Maps have been used since the beginning of time, so don't think you are too good for them or don't need them. You do! Even though maps are available in all kinds of electronic formats these days, don't depend on that. A good set of hard copy maps are indispensable. A full-sized road atlas should be kept in your bugout vehicle, and at least one pocket-sized road atlas should be stored away in your primary bugout bag. If you want to be ahead of the game, you should have your potential bugout locations and routes already planned out on your maps. This will avoid the last minute, 'Which way do I go?' when the time comes.

Compass - So how many people actually know how to use a compass? Do you think it is about time you learn? The simple compass can mean the difference between you living and dying. Getting a bearing on direction is a vital skill that must be learned and learned well. Compasses come in both traditional style and electronic. Learn the traditional one because electronics may not work. Unless the planet's magnetic poles shift soon (and if they do we have much, much bigger problems), the traditional compass will also let you establish what direction is north, south, east and west. So learn basic compass navigation.

GPS - Global positioning systems are like a map AND a compass in a box. They are great if you can depend on them. They make getting from here to there easier than waking up in the morning. However, they depend on: several dozen satellites in space working at all times, service that is always available and no one (probably the government) deciding to turn off access to the general public. These are some big assumptions in times of crisis. So should you have them? Absolutely, put them in every car. It is just downright convenient. But don't let them supersede your other navigational methods. A GPS comes in two main categories: on road navigation and off road navigation. The kind you have in your car is based around road, highways, addresses, etc. These are fine, but have a portable, hand-held GPS, as well, that can be used to chart terrain, waterways, lakes and nature in general. This is what you will want when navigating back woods areas. You may need to be staying off of the roads at some point. However, with either variety I only recommend one company: Garmin.

Watch - Most people don't think of a watch as a great navigational tool; but they are wrong. Some of today's watches are solar powered, utilize an atomic clock, are waterproof and can contain an electronic compass, barometer, altimeter, thermometer, stopwatch, timer and sun and moon phase calculator (and yes, even tell the date and time)! A fine line of these outdoor watches is the Casio Pro Trek series. Even without one of these bad boys, you can still use a standard analog watch to find your basic bearings by utilizing the watch method. Make sure your watch is set to standard time and not daylight savings time. The steps of this method are as follows:

1. Hold the watch horizontally and point the hour hand at the sun.
2. Bisect the angle between the hour hand and the 12 o'clock mark on the dial. This point running through the center of the watch dial is your rough north-south line.
3. If you have a problem determining which way is north and which way is south, just remember that the sun rises in the east and sets in the west. The sun is in the east before noon and in the west after noon.

Sun and Stars - The sun and the heavens have been used by navigators since ancient times. I am going to demonstrate one method, for determining direction, using the sun and one method using a star. The method using the sun is known as the shadow tip method. All you need for this is a simple straight stick, approximately 1 to 2 feet long, and a clear area exposed to the direct sunlight. The steps to this method are as follows:

1. Place the stick into the ground so that its tip can cast a shadow. Mark the shadow's tip on the ground with a rock or some other small object.
2. Wait 15 to 30 minutes until the shadow's tip has moved a short distance. Mark the new tip with another rock or other object as you did with the first one.
3. Draw a straight line through the two marks to create an

approximate east-west line.

4 . Stand so that your left foot is pointed at the first mark and your right foot is pointed at the second mark. You are now facing north.

The method to determine north, using the stars, is easy but must be done at night. Are you ready for this? Find the north star, Polaris. You've now found north! Now I am not going to give you a whole astronomy lesson on how to find the north star. That will be your homework. But I will give you a hint: the north star is directly halfway between the constellations of the Big Dipper and Cassiopeia. So go find it as a family.

Electrical Tape - Finally, I am going to share a method which I have used, to not necessarily show me a direction, but rather, to mark my trail as to where I have been, sort of Hansel and Gretel style. For this, you will need a multi-pack of different colored electrical tape from the hardware store. These usually come in 6 different colors. This is a great item to have for many reasons. The method is as follows: as I am walking through the woods, or any other place I might get turned around or lost, I mark my location about every 50 to 100 yards. I do this with a small piece of electrical tape which I consistently put in the same location, such as the tip of a low hanging branch clearly in sight. Now this is important. I always keep the colored tapes in order and rotate through them in the same order as I go, never using the same color tape in a row to mark. In other words, if I have six colors, one of which is blue, I will only use blue every sixth time that I mark. This way, if I get turned around, all I have to do is find a previous mark, search and locate the next closest one and I can always know what direction I was heading, based on the colors and which direction I came from. It works beautifully, and no, I don't care about littering at this point. I care about survival.

Signaling Methods

In certain emergency scenarios when you can't dial 911, you

might need to desperately attract the attention of a needed rescue party over a great distance, or maybe just covertly relay a simple message to a person a few hundred yards away. Either way, signaling is a valuable survival skill which can take many forms. Some signals are mainly for nighttime usage, whereas others are seen better during daylight hours. Other things that can play into effective signaling include distance, and weather conditions, along with available light. Signals can be visual based, sound based or a combination of the two. Having a good assortment of signaling methods available for various conditions is always a solid recommendation and an approach that should be followed. Some of the most common signaling methods include:

Signal Fire/Smoke Signal - One of the most basic of signaling methods (usually at night) is the signal fire. A fire in the darkness will quickly attract attention and can be seen from a great distance. If in your situation, this would not be seen as anything particularly unusual (for example, many fires within view), another more eye-catching version of this can be used. In this case, you may want to take something flammable, such as a shirt or towel, and wrap it around the end of a large stick or piece of wood. Light this material on fire, using your main fire, and then begin waving it back and forth in the air to signal your desired target. If it is during the daytime hours, smoke, utilizing the fire, would probably be a better signal. Using your fire, toss it in any material that would produce thick, dark smoke, such as a tire or any other rubber material. Green leaves and vegetation will also produce a good supply of smoke, but be careful not to extinguish your fire.

Flashlights - These are obviously one of your top ten survival items for obvious reasons, one of which is their signaling ability. Flashlights can be seen easily at night and can either produce a solid, continuous beam or can be turned on and off to use visual codes, such as morse code or other prearranged signals. Do not skimp on your flashlights. They can come as battery powered models or as crank models. I would suggest having several of both. My recommendations for the battery powered manufacturers are SureFire or Streamlight.

Strobe Lights - Strobe lights give off single flashes of light at various frequencies. Most are adjustable so that the flash can either be slow and steady or rapid fire, depending on your need. Some can be in other colors as well as white light. All need to be waterproof since they may be used as beacons on land or sea. Whereas flashlights can be operated to act as strobes, the actual strobe lights can be turned on and left to strobe the light, totally on their own for long periods of time. The two actual products I recommend, in this area, are the Streamlight Sidewinder and the Princeton Tec Aqua Strobe.

Cyalume (Chemical Light) Sticks - These use a chemical mixture, that when combined through bending, cracking and shaking, creates a fluorescent glow that can last from 8 to 12 hours. These light sticks come in a variety of colors and sizes and are excellent for marking things (or people) at night, as many of you know from your little tots trick or treating at Halloween. These are one time use items which will expire over time, so this stock has to be constantly maintained.

Whistles - Whistles are lifesavers and they're cheap. So every personal bugout bag should have at least one whistle in them. They can be used to warn, to whistle specific signals such as morse code, to call for help or to just signal someone within sound range (which can be quite far). A good, loud whistle can be a lot better than you just puckering your lips and blowing. So save your breathe. Some of the best and loudest whistles on the market are Storm whistles and the JetScream whistle by Ultimate Survival Technologies.

Air Horns - There's loud and then there's loud. Air horns tend to be extremely loud. These horns use compressed air to generate the sound that can be heard over great distances. While most tend to be one time use items (once the canister is exhausted, you must get another one), nowadays, you can get rechargeable canisters. This means that you only have to buy one air horn, and you can recharge the air supply by using a simple air compressor or bicycle pump.

Signal Mirrors - Signal mirrors can be used during the day to get the attention of someone on the ground, or in the air, such as a passing airplane. While there are many manufacturers of ready-made signal mirrors, they can be made, as well, from just about any highly reflective material. Take a flat piece of reflective material (you could use some aluminum foil wrapped around a piece of cardboard, for example) and poke a hole through the center. Now look through the hole in the direction of the sun. Tilt the reflector downward until a bright flash of light is viewable on the ground. Now slowly tilt the reflector up until the flash of light is on the object that you are trying to signal. Tilting back and forth, slightly, can gain the attention of your target.

Signal Flares - These are pyrotechnic devices which can either be held or launched into the air to provide a very bright light and other potential effect for a short time. These are highly portable and range from the simple road flares that you use after a traffic accident, to aerial flare guns, to pocket launchers, to parachute flares, etc. They are basically fireworks on the go and often have loud, whistling noises or bangs to accompany the illumination effect. Few things will get the more attention than signal flares.

Ground Signals - Never underestimate the power of simple ground signals to let people know where you have been or where you are going. Sometimes, if you want people to find you, it is best to leave behind some obvious and well-placed signs to help them along. One such method is to take a brightly colored shirt or other material and stretch it over some sticks or a bush that is on the path. This lets them know that you have been there. It would be even better to do the same thing, again, further down the path that you are traveling. This way, they not only know that you have been there, but now they also know which direction you are traveling. If you are doing this, stick to the direction that you have indicated; otherwise, you are misleading your followers and will likely throw them off your trail. Another method is to simply gather up 10 to 12 sizable rocks and arrange them in the shape of an arrow, indicating which direction you are traveling. Once again, doing this multiple times during your journey will make it much easier for people to locate you, if that is your wish.

Tips

Basic

- Sometimes it is easier to call long distance rather than locally during an emergency, so make sure you have a contact person outside your area who can be a point person if needed.
- Even though your cell phone service may not be going through, often times text messaging will still work.
- Keep your maps in a waterproof bag.
- Avoid blowing whistles except in an emergency.
- State line welcome centers give out complimentary maps. Take them.
- Cyalume light sticks expire over time, so let your kids play with the old ones each Halloween and use this time to replenish your supply. This way you always have fresh ones each year.
- Make sure you have enough 2-way handheld radios so that each person has one in their personal bugout bags. Make sure everyone knows what channel will be used to make initial contact when needed.
- Blowing your whistle or other audio device three times is a universal call for help.
- Only use your emergency cell phone when it is actually an emergency so that it will be ready when the time comes. Turn it off when not in use.

Do Now!

- Talk with family members or others that you would be bugging out with, and come up with an agreed upon, written communications plan.

- Make sure everyone has a hard copy emergency contact list with phone numbers, email addresses and physical addresses.
- Learn to use a compass for navigation.
- Obtain free maps from your auto insurance carrier.
- Have everyone in your family, who has a cell phone, use the ICE (In Case of Emergency) method, by creating a contact labeled 'ICE'. This should contain the phone number of the person, who needs to be contacted, should they be injured or cannot respond.
- Become a licensed HAM radio operator.
- Begin teaching yourself and your family about the stars and where they are located in different seasons. Be sure to be able to recognize Polaris, the north star. This can be a great family fun activity.
- Find a list of all your police and other emergency scanner codes. Laminate it and put in with your other communications gear in your supplies.
- Post an emergency contact list on your refrigerator.
- Take your family out geocaching with your GPS. It is a lot of fun for the family and helps teach basic navigation and GPS usage.
- Print out a copy of morse code letters and numbers; laminate and keep in your supplies.
- Agree upon three different meeting points in case of an emergency: one in a neighborhood, one in a community, and one at least 50 miles from a community. Write these down along with planned routes, and make sure all members have a copy.

Checklist

Communications / Navigation / Signaling Items

(In no particular order)

- Cyalume light sticks (minimum 8 hour capacity)(multiple colors)
- Emergency whistle (1 per person)(Storm or Ultimate Survival Technologies)
- Two-way radios (1 per person)(Midland or Motorola)(AA battery only)
- Signal mirror w/case
- Shake flashlights (at least 2 per family)(1 per person preferable)
- Flashlights (heavy-duty)(AA or lithium battery only)(SureFire or Streamlight recommended)
- Aerial flare kit
- Emergency crank shortwave radio w/cell phone charger and NOAA channels (Eton)
- Electrical tape (assorted colors)
- Strobe light (Princeton Tec Aqua Strobe or Streamlight Sidewinder)
- Emergency cell phone (Tracfone)
- Crank flashlight
- CB radio (Midland or Cobra)
- Headlamps (AA battery only)
- Emergency scanners (Uniden)
- Spotlight
- HAM radio (Yaesu, Kenwood, Icom or Alinco)
- Handheld GPS (Garmin)(AA battery only)
- Wristwatch (solar/atomic/barometer/compass/thermometer)(Casio Pro Trek)
- Military style lensatic compass

Ch 7 - General

Now that we come to chapter 7, there are still things which do not fit directly into the six categories that have preceded. Therefore, we have created a catch-all, general chapter to pick up any loose slack. However, do not be mistaken, this may be the most important chapter of all. The reality is that it takes a lot of different things to survive in an emergency situation. No one can possibly plan for them all. That is the dichotomy of preparedness: you prepare for situations that you are aware of, or at least can comprehend, but a true emergency might be something that you have no previous experience with. It might come totally out of the blue and hit you broadside. We can't think of it all, but we prepare the best we can.

Techniques

Vehicle Considerations

When it comes to gathering up last minute supplies at the time of an emergency, or gathering up scattered family members or just getting out of Dodge when you need to, none of these things will happen if your vehicle is not in prime working condition. Granted, a clunker is better than nothing, but you need that clunker in the best state possible, or you will find yourself with few options available. So if you are limited by what you have currently and will be in the market for a new vehicle in the months to come, take note of these suggestions.

Obviously given the fact that preparing for mobility is the best option (even if you don't have to use it), the point of your main bugout vehicle is to move as much needed supplies from point A to point B in a timely fashion. While some of the vehicle considerations mentioned below will obviously not accomplish this task adequately on their own, they still deserve mention due to other factors.

4x4 Truck - This is by far my preferred bugout vehicle for several reasons. First, a 4x4 truck has the ability to go where other vehicles might be otherwise restricted. Sometimes, it might be necessary to travel off road to get to secluded areas or to bypass certain traffic congestion areas. There is power in a truck, and power is often what you need. Secondly, trucks have greater towing capacity and winch capability. Since you have gone to the trouble to collect all these supplies, you will need to get them to your destination. Often this will mean towing trailers, boats, campers or other units. Also, whether you are traveling in a single bugout vehicle or multiple vehicles, you or someone else might easily get stuck and need to be pulled free. The winch can be a lifesaver in this situation and can also give you the ability to help others, if needed. Thirdly, people will tend to mess less with you in a truck than in a Ford Focus, so to speak. I call that the truck intimidation factor. No one wants to mess with a good ole country boy who is probably well armed.

All-wheel Drive Car, Jeep or Van - The next best thing to a 4x4 truck would be an all-wheel drive car, jeep or van; however, with this type of vehicle you are most likely sacrificing a lot of towing capacity (which in turn means a lot of supply carrying capacity), especially with cars or jeeps. While these vehicles might be labeled all-terrain, or something similar, the reality is that they are usually much lower to the ground, compared to a truck, and therefore easily stranded in an off road situation. The exception to this might be the jeep. When selecting from this category, you should try to get one with a towing capacity of at least 3500 pounds. These will usually be in the SUV or van categories.

Motorcycle - I am sure you have already figured out that a motorcycle would make a horrible primary bugout vehicle and you are right. While great on gas and maneuverability, it has extremely limited person and supply carrying capacity. The reason it is mentioned here is this: if it were able to be accommodated on or in a trailer, it could prove a fine asset to have along. This would give you a good mode of quick and cheap transportation to use as a recon vehicle from your primary bugout location. However, it is loud and can be heard from great distances, which is sometimes not desired.

Bicycle - A highly stealthy mode of transportation which can save you a lot of walking time is the common bicycle. It also allows you to be a little faster than the potential thug on foot. I would highly advise including at least one mountain bike in your supplies, if you can fit it, in the back of a truck or in a trailer. Be sure you have a spare chain and a tire repair kit as well.

Camper or Mobile Home - The benefits of a camper or mobile home are that you can fit a lot in them and have your basic home and shelter travel with you. The practical drawback is that, in a crisis situation when gas is at a premium, you may not be driving far or long. Mobile homes are notorious for poor gas mileage. When the gas runs out, the home stays put wherever that might be. However, a camper pulled behind your primary bugout vehicle might be an excellent choice. The camper would need to be a full upright camper instead of a pop-up so that more supplies could be stored in it.

Trailer - As opposed to a camper, you don't get an equipped shelter with an enclosed trailer, but you do get a lot of storage capacity. You would be surprised how much an enclosed 5x8, 6x10 or 7x14 foot trailer can hold. A trailer also gives you the advantage of using it as your supply base of operations, and if you can keep it packed with your supplies hidden within your garage, you have a quick method of going mobile in a very short period of time.

Boat - When having to choose between what to tow in an emergency, a camper, an enclosed trailer or a boat, the boat usually will come in third. However, there are situations and bugout locations where a boat may make sense. If you have a lake house, for example, and already have most of your supplies stored there, perhaps towing a boat at the last minute would be a good move.

With any of these vehicles, it is of vital importance that they be maintained and in excellent working order. If they utilize a tire, make sure you have a good spare one for backup. Also, make sure you have any needed supplies to make minor repairs, such as jacks, lug nuts, tire tools, extra oil, etc. All tags and inspections should be up to date, too. I have included a vehicle supply checklist and a tool checklist at the end of the chapter. In an emergency, mobility matters. It should matter to you.

Storing Your Stuff

What can I say about storing your stuff? A lot! This could be, perhaps, one of the most important sections in this book. Even with the people who claim that they are prepared for an emergency, if I walked into their home and named a vital supply item (which they had!), they would probably take 30 to 45 minutes to find it. The sad reality is that most people are not organized, and a disaster survival situation is no time to be trying to remember where you last saw the sleeping bags. The simple reality check I like to ask is this: If someone knocked on your door out of the blue, and told you that you needed to leave your house and never return, how quickly could you round everything up and be on the road with all your necessary supplies? If your truthful answer is, "within 6 hours", then you are better than 99% out there but still not acceptable. If your answer is, "less than 2 hours", then you are definitely getting in the ballpark and have some good organizational skills. If you say, "within 1 hour", then you are my kind of person and I salute you. However, with my family, my goal has always been 30 minutes. Yes, you heard me right, 30 minutes! That's 30 minutes to be loaded into the truck, be towing the trailer with all my supplies and be heading down the back roads - figuratively waving at all the others scrambling to head to the hardware and grocery store or standing in line waiting for gasoline.

In order for you to even come close to these figures, you would need to have all your supplies stored in as few locations as possible, preferably a single location such as a spare bedroom, a large walk-in closet or the garage. While good organization in this area could get you closer to the 2 hour mark, you would still have to load all your supplies into your vehicle before you were able to turn the key, start the engine and head off. This could take considerable time and energy. The ideal situation would be to have all your supplies pre-bagged (will explain later) and pre-loaded into your trailer in the garage. Some temperature-sensitive items would have to be left out during the hot months; however, these should still be stored in a single location, during this time, for easy access. This way, when short notice is given, you simply back the truck up, connect the hitch, gather the few (and I mean few) remaining items from the home, tell the kids and the family dog to get in and make your move.

With that said, obviously the better your individual items are organized, grouped and stored in manageable fewer units, the better. It is a lot easier to lift and move 3 bags, containing 50 items each, around rather than to individually move all 150 items separately. So pay very close attention to the remainder of this section.

Duffle Bags - Duffle bags are your friend! I repeat, duffle bags are your friend! Use them, and use lots of them. Military-style, canvas, duffle bags have been used by the armed forces for centuries. They work well. Whether it is a top loading or a side loading bag, they serve a vital role in your preparations, are relatively cheap and come in various shapes, colors and sizes. How you organize, within the duffle bags, is a personal preference. Some people organize by a survival area - such as a primary first aid bag, or a shelter/tent bag, or a vehicle supply bag, or a pots/pans bag or a tool bag. Others just throw various things into each bag to distribute the weight and functionality. Do with it what you will. Army surplus stores or sporting goods stores will generally have a large supply.

Personal Bugout Bags/Backpacks - These bags serve a very specialized purpose, and I put a little more emphasis on their high quality and durability. To explain, I group all your supplies into three levels: Level I, Level II and Level III. Level I is defined by the question: If your family had to leave with only one bag for the entire group, which could be carried by a single individual, what would it be? This I refer to as your primary bugout bag. It is usually carried and is the responsibility of the leader of the group. Level II is defined by the question: If your family had to leave with only one bag each, which could be carried by that member, what would it be? This I refer to as the individual or personal bugout bag. Therefore, the leader has the primary bugout bag, and the other persons have their own personal bugout bags. (I have an example below, of some suggested contents) Level III is all the other supplies and bags. This means that you prepare as if your primary bugout bag and your personal bugout bags could be the only things you actually leave with; therefore, you want these to be long-lasting and of high quality. These could be as simple as kids' school-type backpacks, but hiking backpacks or military style patrol packs would serve much better. Companies that I recommend in this area include: The North Face, Kelty, High Sierra and Blackhawk.

Rubberized Storage Containers/Bins - These come in all shapes and sizes and are great for holding everything from food stuffs, to canned goods, to clothing to just about anything. They should be easy to lift and be durable enough to hold whatever you plan on putting into them. Most should come with a lid and be able to be stacked, when necessary. The brand that comes to mind that makes excellent products in this area is Rubbermaid.

5 Gallon Plastic Buckets - As seen in the chapter on food and nutrition, food grade 5 gallon buckets are wonderful when it comes to storing bulk staple foods such as rice, beans, wheat, corn, flour, etc. But apart from that, they serve an endless amount of duties ranging from water gathering, to portable toilet, to supply storage, to makeshift sink, to seat, to fish bucket and beyond. These buckets also stack really well, are very strong and are easily handled. One place where I have gotten exceptional products in this area is ULine.

No matter which storage device you end up utilizing, always label or number it and record its contents, including when things expire. By keeping a complete inventory of what you have and where it is stored, you will save hours of unnecessary hunting and searching when the time comes. I suggest that you keep the master inventory document among your vital papers and stored within the primary bugout bag, as described further down.

Now I want to say a few words about your Level I primary bugout bag and your Level II personal bugout bags. Given that you may escape your emergency or disaster situation (no matter what it is) with no more than the single Level I bag or the Level I and Level

II bags together, you need to make wise choices as to what goes into these particular bugout bags. You should have items in each bag that cover each of the main areas of need. These are detailed in chapters 1 through 6. Put a lot of thought into what is going in each of these bags. These bags should be kept up to date and stored very near an appropriate exit, should you need to grab nothing but this and flee, as in the case of a fire. Below, I am going to give you an example of some contents for the primary and personal bugout bags. This is only a suggestion, and you need to think about your own personal situation. Everything mentioned in this example has already been accounted for in the checklists of this book. Utilize all room in these bags. Fill them to the capacity that the person can carry comfortably. This may be all you get.

EXAMPLE ONLY

Primary Bugout Bag - vital documents in waterproof bag, extra set of house and bugout vehicle keys, pistol and ammo, stun gun, retractable metal baton, zip ties, wire snips, handcuffs, knife, knife sharpener, Katadyn Pocket Filter, SteriPEN, LifeSaver bottle, 3 day supply of water, 3 days of MRE rations, emergency survival tabs, energy bars, emergency space blanket, inflatable pillow, eating utensil set, chow set, cook set, spatula, spoon, whisk, cast net, snares, esbit pocket stove, magnesium fire starter, can opener, 550 parachord, emergency candles, holiday jingle bells, fishing line, fishing rod and reel, fishing tackle, snares, carabiner, multi-tool, cash and change, waterproof notebook and pen, toothpaste and toothbrush, crank lantern, waterproof fire sticks, work gloves, pocket atlas, toilet paper, wool blanket, rain poncho, 2 yo-yo fishing reels, emergency tent, large first aid kit, field hatchet, machete, shovel/entrenching tool, BlastMatch, SabreCut survival saw, cyalume light sticks, emergency whistle, two-way radio, signal mirror, flashlight, batteries, 4 garbage bags, aerial flare kit, crank shortwave radio, emergency cell phone, emergency scanner, handheld GPS, electrical tape, compass, duct tape, assault climbing rope, military sewing kit, harmonica, binoculars, roll of thin wire, single sided razor blades, army survival manual, first aid manual, caffeine pills, extra set of clothes, 2 pairs of dry socks, 2 pairs of underwear, anything else you can fit - especially food

Personal Bugout Bag(s) - pocket knife, pepper spray, LifeStraw, Katadyn MyBottle, 3 day supply of water, eating utensil set, chow set, emergency can opener, 2 days of MRE rations, emergency survival tabs, energy bars, emergency space blanket, inflatable pillow, disposable lighter, magnesium fire starter, toilet paper, wool blanket, emergency tent, small first aid kit, cyalume light sticks, emergency whistle, two-way radio, signal mirror, flashlight, shake flashlight, 2 garbage bags, fishing line, batteries, carabiner, multi-tool, waterproof bag, playing cards, nylon rope, cash and change, waterproof notebook and pen, reusable hand warmer, toothpaste and toothbrush, compass, rain poncho, 2 yo-yo fishing reels, fishing rod and reel, light fishing tackle, snares, extra set of clothes, 2 pairs of dry socks, 2 pairs of underwear, anything else you can fit

Tips

Basic

○ Make sure anything you buy, that needs batteries, uses either AA or 123A Lithium only.
○ Entertainment, especially for kids, will be of vital importance. Pack some items which can provide hours of entertainment for all. Make sure they are small and light-weight such as playing cards, sock puppets and harmonicas.
○ In a survival situation, remember the rule of 3s: a person can live roughly 3 hours without maintaining their core body temperature, 3 days without water and 3 weeks without food. Therefore, the order of priority should be: shelter, water and then food.
○ Keep a separate bugout bag packed with a single set of environment-appropriate clothes for each member, just in case you are forced to flee in the middle of the night.

o Checklists are vital. Use them to stay organized.
o Layering of clothes is a good idea for a survival situation. This gives you greater flexibility to shed layers, as well as a good insulation barrier between layers.
o Bandannas are great for many purposes: from dust masks, to bandages, to head coverings, to wash cloths, to tourniquets, to signaling tools, to basic neck protections and much more.
o When an emergency is unfolding, make sure everyone has their shoes on. Climbing through debris is not advised in bare feet.
o Dry grass, leaves, paper, cattails, animal hair or moss can be packed between clothing layers to provide needed insulation.
o If you are traveling any substantial distance away from your home, be sure to take, in your vehicle, your primary and personal bugout bags - in case an emergency situation occurs while you are away from home.
o Always keep your gas level, in all your vehicles, at least half full. As soon as it reaches half empty or before, fill it up. This way if you need to leave in a hurry, you can siphon the gas out of all your extra vehicles and put it into your primary bugout vehicle.
o When it comes to clothing, you should try to get things that are as light as possible, quick drying, easy to care for, low in bulk, breathable and, most importantly, durable.
o Always wear clean and dry socks. If they get wet, replace them immediately.
o Do not depend on hotel/motels during a bugout situation. They will probably be filled or not available.
o Always wear a hat in cold weather, since most heat loss occurs from your head.
o A duffle bag should be stored in your vehicle which contains all necessary vehicle supplies as well as some other basic survival necessities such as blankets, whistle, rain ponchos, small first aid kit, energy bars, etc.
o If you decide you need to bugout, the earlier the better.
o Keep everything packed away until you need it. This way, it will be quickly accessed if you need to leave in a hurry and help prevent the loss of equipment.

- The horizon is generally about 12 miles away when standing on flat ground.
- Every person should have their own personal bugout bag.
- Guard your vehicle keys or at least have a secondary set in a secure and known location. You don' t want to be looking for keys when it is time to go.
- Make a second set of your primary bugout vehicle and house keys, and keep them in your primary bugout bag.
- When drying your boots or shoes at a campsite, place them upside down on sticks that are stuck in the ground. This prevents critters from crawling into them or animals carrying them off.

Do Now!

- Call local thrift stores and ask them about any sales coming up. They often have clothes that they are just getting rid of or are incredibly priced, like $1 for an article or perhaps a complete bag of clothes. You can often find great deals on other items too, such as blankets, cast-iron cookware, fatigues, backpacks, etc.
- Also keep an eye on Craigslist for free stuff that you can use.
- Put $10 to $20 each payday into your safe at home, or with your vital documents, so this will be available during an emergency.
- Get two containers (perhaps 3-liter plastic soda bottles with a large opening that can fit a silver dollar), and begin collecting change. In one bottle, put all silver coins dated 1964 or earlier; in the other, place all other change except for pennies.
- Make a list of actions you need to take in order to secure your home, should you have to leave.
- Pay off your credit cards and get out of debt as much as possible; however, keep a couple of credit cards, with zero balances, in your emergency supplies just in case you need them for a survival situation.
- Keep your bugout vehicle clean of any unnecessary junk.

- Start collecting small film canisters. These can serve a variety of useful purposes.
- Learn to tie various basic knots including the bowline, square knot, trucker's hitch, figure-eight, taut-line hitch, overhand, prusik hitch, butterfly and clove hitch. This is a lot of fun to do with kids and is a valuable skill.
- Have your grown family members participate in a local CERT (Community Emergency Response Teams) training course.
- Get off of the TV and computer, and get your family into the outdoors. Explore the outdoors together and make it a fun and learning experience. In other words, get a real life.
- Break in your boots now before they are needed. Wear them now until they are very comfortable and soft.
- Have your children participate in groups such as Boys or Girl Scouts, 4-H, FFA, Camp Fires or Indian Guides so they can learn and enjoy valuable skills such as camping, cooking, gardening, caring for animals, sewing, etc.
- Make sure your spare tire for you bugout vehicle is fully inflated and in proper condition.
- Start going to garage sales on a regular basis. It is amazing what you can find there inexpensively.
- Have a reasonable amount of cash on hand and stored away for emergencies. In a crisis, ATMs may not work.
- Frequently check tire pressures, including spare tires in your vehicles and make sure they are what they need to be.
- Make a list of all the items you should carry with you at all times, and then do it.
- Hold evacuation drills with your family at least once a year. Show them their quickest way to exit the house in the case of a fire or imminent danger, grabbing a basic bugout bag on the way out. In the case of a longer time to evacuate, show them their responsibilities for quickly gathering necessary items and preparing to leave. Do not make these practices a scary experience.
- The next time you spend the night at a hotel, ask for any complimentary items such as sewing kits, soaps, shampoos, etc. These are great for your bugout bags.
- Place all your important and vital documents into a waterproof

bag.
- Know where the nearest military bases, nuclear facilities, hospitals, campgrounds, chemical plants and national/state parks are.

Checklist

General Items

(In no particular order)

- ○ BATTERIES (AA and lithium only)(a lot)
- ○ Garbage bags (heavy-duty and kitchen) with twist ties
- ○ Zip lock bags (various sizes)
- ○ Rubber bands (assorted sizes)
- ○ Toothpaste
- ○ Toothbrush w/holder (1 per person, minimum)
- ○ 5-gallon, plastic gas can w/nozzle (several are necessary to hold an extra tank of gas for your escape vehicle)
- ○ NBC gas masks w/filter canisters (1 per person)
- ○ Duct tape, duct tape, duct tape
- ○ Carabiners (heavy-duty)(various sizes)(Petzl or Black Diamond)
- ○ Multi-tool (Leatherman or Gerber)
- ○ Bungee cords (assorted lengths)
- ○ Disposable ear plugs
- ○ S-biners, knotbones, figure 9s (various sizes)(NiteIze)
- ○ Assault/climbing rope (50′ minimum)
- ○ Waterproof bags (assorted sizes)
- ○ Inflatable raft
- ○ Playing cards (several decks)
- ○ Geiger counter
- ○ Trekking pole
- ○ Military sewing kit
- ○ EzAdjust rope adjusters
- ○ Backpacks (BlackHawk, Kelty, High Sierra or The North Face)
- ○ Power inverter
- ○ Binoculars
- ○ Spare set of glasses or contact lenses
- ○ Roll of thin wire
- ○ Clothes pins
- ○ Surveyor′s tape (50 foot)

- Pocket Road Atlas
- Single sided razor blades
- Sports tape (several rolls)
- CASH and CHANGE (as much as you can!)
- FM 21-76 Army Survival Manual
- Waterproof notebook and pen (Rite in the Rain)
- Reusable hand warmers
- Dry box (Pelican)
- Harmonica
- Glue sticks
- Military style canvas duffle bags (various sizes)
- Condoms
- Rubber gear Wrapz
- Vivarin caffeine pills
- Nail clippers
- Camouflage tarp (can be used to conceal vehicle, supplies, etc)
- Books (especially the Bible)
- Toys and games (smaller is better)
- Baby diapers (if needed)
- Sand (at least one, 50-pound bag)
- Feminine hygiene products (include cloth ones that you can wash)
- Nylon rope (1/4″)(at least 500 feet)
- Sturdy emergency bicycle
- Fire extinguisher (for shelter/habitat)

Needed Clothing

Clothing for a survival situation is a tricky thing to define, given that every climate and geographical region may have its own requirements. Obviously, hot temperate environments need less, in the way of clothing, than do colder environments; however, always prepare for an environment that is 20 to 30 degrees lower than the lowest yearly temperature in your area. This is in case of some catastrophic weather-changing event, such as a volcanic eruption or a nuclear event, which could throw up large quantities of debris into the atmosphere, thereby blocking out the heat of the sun. I know it is a long shot, but that is what preppers do; we take into consideration the long shots, too. I am listing clothing items here which you should weigh into your own environmental situation to determine what is best for you. Hopefully, some of these items will set the proverbial light bulb off in your head.

- Winter coat (waterproof)(The North Face or Columbia)
- Thermal underwear top/bottom (silk or wool)
- Baseball cap
- Boonie Hat
- Neck gaiter
- Rain jacket
- Rain poncho (1 per person)
- Work Gloves
- Belt
- Cold weather gloves w/liners
- BDUs
- Socks (preferably wool)
- Turtlenecks
- Balaclava
- Sunglasses
- Gaiters
- Rain pants
- Shirts
- Cargo pants
- T-shirts
- Underwear
- Jeans
- Goggles
- Snowshoes
- Pants
- Crampons
- Bandannas (at least a dozen)
- Jacket (waterproof)(The North Face or Columbia)
- Earmuffs
- Boots w/extra laces (with room for heavy socks)
- Sweater (wool or fleece)

- Scarf
- Winter stocking cap
- Athletic shoes w/extra laces
- Extra buttons (various sizes)

Vehicle Supplies

Vehicle supplies are as follows:

- 1-gallon, plastic gas can w/nozzle (keep empty)
- Booster cables (heavy-duty)
- Towing strap (15 foot)
- Automobile hose clamp
- Tire gauge
- Fix-a-flat
- Road atlas (full-size)
- Air compressor w/tire gauge (Superflow Model MV-50)
- Fire extinguisher (for vehicle)
- Tire repair kit
- Spare lug nuts (at least 2)
- Emergency road flares
- Siphon/pump and hoses (for fuel)
- Pair of leather work gloves
- Extra quart or two of engine oil
- Ice scraper and snow brush
- Flashlight (for vehicle)(AA battery) w/extra batteries
- Roll of duct tape
- Tire jack and wrench
- Spare tire (preferably full-size)(excellent condition)
- Work rags
- Tire chains
- Wool blanket (1 per each potential passenger)

Don't Forget The Tools

Tools are as follows:

- Needle nose pliers w/wire cutter
- Hammer
- File
- Screwdrivers (phillips and flathead)(various sizes)
- Screws and nails (various sizes)
- Locking pliers (various sizes)(Vice-Grip)
- Utility knife
- Crowbar
- Field machete (Gerber)
- Hacksaw w/extra blades
- Bolt cutters (heavy-duty)
- Rubber mallet
- Splitting wedge/maul
- Ratchet set
- Tape measure
- Extension cords (100 foot heavy-duty)(at least 2)
- Adjustable wrench (various sizes)
- Allen wrench set

Vital Documents

It is very important that you gather up all important documents into a single location, preferably into a waterproof bag, and store them in the main bugout bag. This insures that, if in a hurry, these will be part of the items which you can quickly depart with. People tend to have vital documents stored all over the place. You don't want to be like ordinary people. Here is a partial list of things which you will want to be a part of these documents:

- Birth certificates
- Social security cards
- Car titles

- Other vehicle titles
- Home mortgage/deed
- Other property mortgages/deeds
- Latitude and longitude of home and other properties
- Medical/dental insurance policy cards
- Life insurance policy cards
- Adoption records
- Military separation papers
- List of all investment account numbers
- Copies of front/back of each credit card
- List of account numbers, phone numbers and balances of all creditors
- Copies of wills and any other legal documents
- Phone and address contact list including family, friends, employers, neighbors, lawyers, physicians and hospitals
- Marriage licenses / divorce decrees
- List of current medications and prescriptions, with current dose and pharmacy
- Copies of drivers licenses
- List of retirement/pension account numbers
- Diplomas and certifications of completion
- Inventory document of all supplies, including what bag (location) they are in (include expiration dates of anything that expires)
- Passports / visas
- Medical history of each person, including shot/immunization records
- Income tax returns (at least the last 3 years)
- Maps with planned routes to various bugout locations
- Instruction manuals or directions for any supply you may have (if needed)
- A recent photograph of each person
- List of potential bugout locations with latitude/longitude
- List of all bank account numbers
- Address and phone numbers of all key local government offices and utilities
- List of all closest military bases/armories with latitude/longitude

○ Any other documents that you feel are vital

If at all possible, scan these documents and keep them on a portable flash usb drive, along with your most treasured family pictures. A second set is always a good thing.

Conclusion - MUST READ!

I can't tell you how many times people, who found out I was preparing, came up to me and said things like, "I want to get prepared too, but I don't know how or where to start," or "I don't have time to do all the research, can you help me?" Well, my friends, this book is for you. This book was never intended to be a full-fledged survival manual (although it has some of that in it). There are plenty of those on the market. Find yourself a good one. It was intended to get you moving, or at the very least: START! This book is about what you can do now, to begin gathering the things you are going to need for when the time comes. The day after chaos breaks out is not the time to be making a trip to the local mall. Preparation means foresight, not hindsight. If this book simply triggered the little light bulb inside your head about something you were lacking in your preparations, or a tip that you hadn't thought about before, then it was well worth my writing and well worth your few dollars.

It may be true that most of you really don't have the luxury of all the time it would take to research all the supply choices. That is why I have given you my recommendations when I felt strongly about a particular product or brand because I have done the research. I have put in the countless hours of trial and error to see what really works and what will hold up when the time comes. I am a husband and father like many of you, and I wouldn't own it if I wasn't going to trust it for its safety. Everything, that was mentioned in this book and that I recommended, I own and trust personally. Many brands and products did not make it into this book because I have tried them and did not have sufficient confidence in their quality or functionality. You bought this book for my expertise, and that is what I gave you. Are there good products that did not make it into the book? I am sure there are some. If you feel led, try them and let me know their results. That brings me to my next point.

This book is a work in progress. It is a living and breathing guide from this day forward. It is your work and your thoughts as well. I want to hear from you: your tips, your techniques and your items. We are in this together. The name of the game is survival, and I want you standing with me when the time comes. This is not a time to think only of yourselves; we can benefit each other. You will not be able to help everyone; some people don't want to be helped or would rather stay oblivious to everything around them. We can continue to pray for those people, but don't be one of those people. I have created a form at www.WhenThingsGoBoom.com where you can send in your tips and ideas. You may have a really interesting tip that no one else has ever thought of. Send it in. If it is a good tip, I will include it in the next version of the book. If you sign up on the site, I will email you groups of new tips that have come in and are worth mentioning. I would love to see this book double or triple in the number of useful tips during the next few months. This brings me to another point.

I have also included on the website an amazon store where I have placed all (or most) of the products which I have recommended throughout this book. If I felt strongly about the product or brand, I tried to put it in there. I also followed the structure of this book in the organization of the products to make it easier for you. Ok, listen to me very carefully. Are you listening? I did NOT write this book or put this store on the site for the primary purpose of making money! I repeat, I did not do that. I wrote this book for the sole purpose of helping people prepare. The store on the website was done as an afterthought so that it would make it easy for my readers to be able to locate, investigate and purchase the supplies that I had recommended. It was done to complement the book. After all, what good is it if I recommend products for you to get, and then make you go through the hassle of finding where to purchase them? That didn't make sense to me. Now I am not going to lie to you. I would be thrilled if you purchased any supplies through my website since it would put a couple of dollars in my pocket to help continue to write this book; however, the important thing is that you get what you need wherever you have to get it. It is not going to cost you any more by going through my website or going directly to the company. In fact, it will most likely be cheaper for you going through my website since most of these items already reflect the lowest price around. Now that that has been said, I want to leave you with a few final words.

Even more than preparation and supplies, survival is a mindset. You must have already made up your mind that you will not be a quitter, if not for yourself, then for your family and friends. The will to survive is a strong force; however, like a light switch, some people can choose to flip it off. I don't do what I do because I fear death. I do what I do because I love life. So the next time a family member or friend comes up to you and asks how they, too, can begin to get prepared, and they want an answer in 5 minutes or less, smile and hand them a copy of the book. You may have just saved their life and they might not even know it. God Bless.

www.WhenThingsGoBoom.com

Appendix: Suggested Vendor Websites

Alinco - www.alinco.com
AlpineAire - www.aa-foods.com
ASP - www.asp-usa.com
ATN - www.atncorp.com
Backpacker's Pantry - www.backpackerspantry.com
Barnett Crossbows - www.barnettcrossbows.com
Bear Archery - www.beararcheryproducts.com
Benelli - www.benelliusa.com
Beretta - www.berettausa.com
Bersa - www.bersa.com
Black Diamond - www.blackdiamondequipment.com
BlackHawk - www.blackhawk.com
Buckshots - www.snare-trap-survive.com
Bullfrog - www.bullfrogsunblock.com
Bushmaster - www.bushmaster.com
CamelBak - www.camelbak.com
Camp Chef - www.campchef.com
Canning Pantry - www.canningpantry.com
Casio - www.casio.com
Char-Broil - www.charbroil.com
Cobra - www.cobra.com
Coghlans - www.coghlans.com
Coleman - www.coleman.com
Columbia - www.columbia.com
Costco - www.costco.com
Crimson Trace - www.crimsontrace.com
Datrex - www.datrex.com
Emmrod - www.emmrod.com
EO-Tech - www.eotech-inc.com
Eureka - www.eurekatent.com
Excalibur Crossbows - www.excaliburcrossbow.com
Excalibur Dehydrator - www.excaliburdehydrator.com
Federal - www.federalpremium.com
Fox Labs - www.foxlabs.com
Gamo - www.gamo.com

Garmin - www.garmin.com
Generac - www.generac.com
Gerber - www.gerbergear.com
Heirloom Organics - www.non-hybrid-seeds.com
Hi-Point Firearms - www.hi-pointfirearms.com
High Sierra - www.hssc.com
Honeyville - www.honeyvillegrain.com
Hornady - www.hornady.com
Icom - www.icomamerica.com
Insight Technology - www.insightlights.com
Ka-Bar - www.kabar.com
Katadyn - www.katadyn.com
Kelty - www.kelty.com
Kenwood - www.kenwoodusa.com
Kershaw - www.kershawknives.com
Leatherman - www.leatherman.com
Leupold - www.leupold.com
LifeSaver - www.lifesaverusa.com
LifeStraw - www.vestergaard-frandsen.com/lifestraw
Mainstay - www.survivorind.com
Marmot - www.marmot.com
Martin Archery - www.martinarchery.com
Midland - www.midlandradio.com
Mora of Sweden - www.moraofsweden.se
Mossberg - www.mossberg.com
Motorola - www.motorola.com
Mountain House - www.mountainhouse.com
Mr Heater - www.mrheater.com
MSR - www.cascadedesigns.com/MSR
Nesco - www.nesco.com
Nikon - www.nikonhunting.com
Nite Ize - www.niteize.com
Pelican - www.pelican.com
Petzl - www.petzl.com
ProCom - www.usaprocom.com
REI - www.rei.com
Remington - www.remington.com
Rite in the Rain - www.riteintherain.com

Rubbermaid - www.rubbermaid.com
Ruger - www.ruger.com
Sabre - www.sabrered.com
Sam's Club - www.samsclub.com
Sawyer - www.sawyer.com
Shelf Reliance - www.shelfreliance.com
Smith & Wesson - www.smith-wesson.com
Snow Peak - www.snowpeak.com
SOG - www.sogknives.com
Solar Oven Society - www.solarovens.org
SOPAKCO - www.sopakco.com
Sorbent Systems - www.sorbentsystems.com
Speer - www.speer-ammo.com
Springfield Armory - www.springfield-armory.com
Sprout People - www.sproutpeople.org
SteriPen - www.steripen.com
Storm - www.stormwhistles.com
Streamlight - www.streamlight.com
Sun Oven - www.sunoven.com
SuperFlow - www.superflowair.com
SureFire - www.surefire.com
Survival Tabs - www.survivaltabs.com
The North Face - www.thenorthface.com
Therm-a-Rest - www.cascadedesigns.com
Timberline - www.gatcosharpeners.com
Tomahawk Live Traps - www.livetrap.com
Trijicon - www.trijicon.com
Troy-Bilt - www.troybilt.com
Uline - www.uline.com
Ultimate Survival Tech - www.ultimatesurvivaltech.com
Uniden - www.uniden.com
Vice-Grip - www.irwin.com
Vogelzang - www.vogelzang.com
WaterBOB - www.waterbob.com
Weber - www.weber.com
Winchester - www.winchester.com
Wise Food Choice - www.wisefoodchoice.com
Wise Food Storage - www.wisefoodstorage.com

WonderMill - www.thewondermill.com
Yaesu - www.yaesu.com

2048360R00074

Printed in Great Britain
by Amazon.co.uk, Ltd.,
Marston Gate.